Chronological and Background Charts
of the
OLD
TESTAMENT

ZondervanCharts Books in the Series

Chronological and Background Charts
of the
OLD
TESTAMENT
Revised and Expanded

John H. Walton

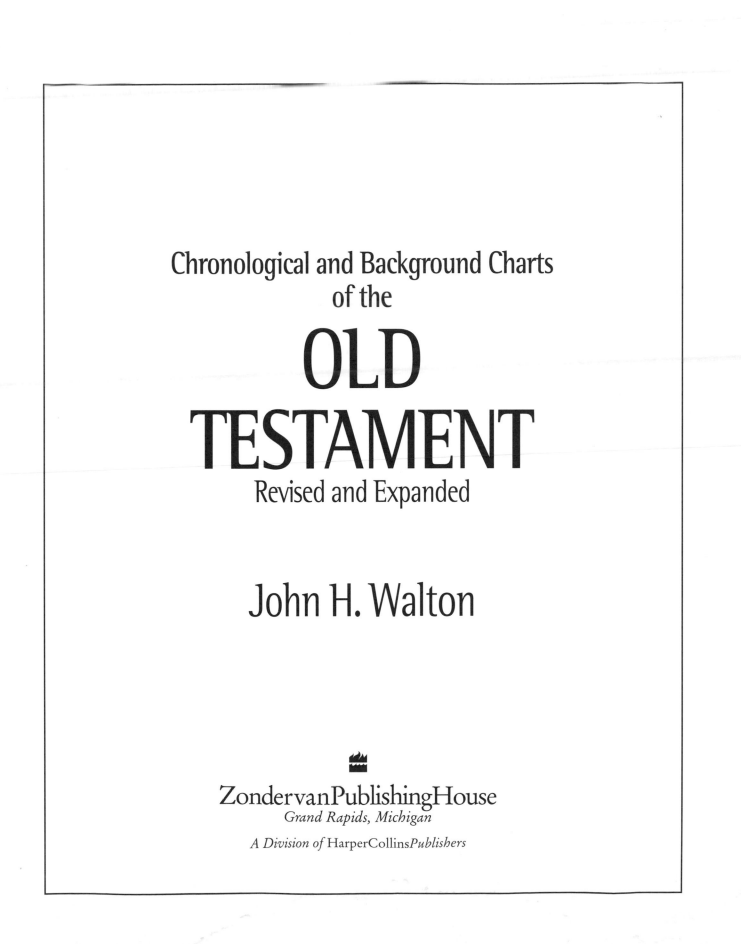

ZondervanPublishingHouse
Grand Rapids, Michigan
A Division of HarperCollinsPublishers

To Kim, with much love

Chronological and Background Charts of the Old Testament, Revised and Expanded
Copyright © 1978, 1994 by John H. Walton

Requests for information should be addressed to:
Zondervan Publishing House
Grand Rapids, Michigan 49530

Library of Congress Cataloging-in-Publication Data

Walton, John H.   1952–
    Chronological and background charts of the Old Testament / John H. Walton.—Rev.
and expanded ed.

        p.   cm.
    ISBN 0-310-48161-9
    1. Bible. O.T.—Chronology.   I. Title.

    BS637.2.W36   1994
    221'.02'02—dc20   94–12748
                                                                          CIP

Printed in the United States of America

99 00 01 02 /❖CH/ 10

Contents

Preface to the Revised Edition

It has been twenty years since I first envisioned a book of charts that would assemble a wide spectrum of material about the Old Testament. I was a graduate student just embarking on my professional career, but it seemed that such a book would serve a helpful purpose for teachers and students alike. The response has overwhelmingly confirmed that my intuition was correct. The appearance of a number of chart books in other areas, many foreign language translations, and more than twenty printings of this volume have been gratifying testimony to the welcome this concept has received.

Even during the first couple of years that this book was on the market, people began to mention that there was a lot more that could be done. Additionally, as I began teaching, I developed more and more material for classroom use. Finally the time has come to expand the original *Chronological and Background Charts of the Old Testament.* This revised edition nearly doubles the number of charts. Of the new charts, several have already appeared in print in the *Survey of the Old Testament* that I published several years ago with Andrew Hill. Many others were put together (e.g., Egyptian Chronology); some reflect a different approach to the material (e.g., Chronology of the Kings of Israel and Judah; Classification of the Psalms).

The charts have been arranged in different categories than in the first edition. I trust that the new arrangement will be found convenient. I have also taken advantage of this opportunity to add a subject index that I think will be useful.

It is my hope and prayer that this new edition will further enhance the reader's understanding of the Old Testament and its background and will increase enthusiasm for the Old Testament as an important segment of God's revelation of himself to us.

John H. Walton
June 1994

I.

Sections of the Canon

The Holy Scriptures

HEBREW NAMES FOR THE BOOKS	HEBREW ARRANGEMENT AND CLASSIFICATION		ENGLISH ARRANGEMENT AND CLASSIFICATION		APPROXIMATE DATES CONCERNED
In the beginning These are the names And He called In the wilderness These are the words	TORAH	Genesis Exodus Leviticus Numbers Deuteronomy	Genesis Exodus Leviticus Numbers Deuteronomy	LAW (Pentateuch)	The Beginning to 1406 B.C.
Joshua Judges I Samuel II Samuel I Kings II Kings	FORMER PROPHETS	Joshua Judges I Samuel II Samuel I Kings II Kings	Joshua Judges Ruth I Samuel II Samuel I Kings II Kings I Chronicles II Chronicles Ezra Nehemiah Esther	HISTORY	1406-1380 B.C. 1380-1050 B.C. 1200-1150 B.C. 1100-1010 B.C. 1010-971 B.C. 971-853 B.C. 853-560 B.C. 1010-971 B.C. 971-539 B.C. 539-450 B.C. 445-410 B.C. 483-474 B.C.
Isaiah Jeremiah Ezekiel Hosea Joel Amos Obadiah Jonah Micah Nahum Habakkuk Zephaniah Haggai Zechariah Malachi	LATTER PROPHETS	Isaiah Jeremiah Ezekiel Hosea Joel Amos Obadiah Jonah Micah Nahum Habakkuk Zephaniah Haggai Zechariah Malachi	Job Psalms Proverbs Ecclesiastes Song of Solomon	POETRY and WISDOM	No specific historical period covered
			Isaiah Jeremiah Lamentations Ezekiel Daniel	MAJOR PROPHETS	739-700 B.C. 627-580 B.C. 586 B.C. 593-570 B.C. 605-530 B.C.
Praises Job Proverbs Ruth Song of Songs The Preacher How! Esther Daniel Ezra Nehemiah I The words of the days II The words of the days	THE WRITINGS (Hagiographa)	Psalms Job Proverbs Ruth Song of Solomon Ecclesiastes Lamentations Esther Daniel Ezra Nehemiah I Chronicles II Chronicles	Hosea Joel Amos Obadiah Jonah Micah Nahum Habakkuk Zephaniah Haggai Zechariah Malachi	MINOR PROPHETS	760-730 B.C. 500 B.C. 760 B.C. 500 B.C. 770 B.C. 737-690 B.C. 650 B.C. 630 B.C. 627 B.C. 520 B.C. 520-518 B.C. 433 B.C.

Genealogies from Adam to Abraham*

Name	AGE AT BIRTH OF SON	YEARS LIVED AFTER BIRTH OF SON	TOTAL YEARS	GENESIS REFERENCE
Adam	130	800	930	5:3-5
Seth	105	807	912	5:6-8
Enosh	90	815	905	5:9-11
Kenan	70	840	910	5:12-14
Mahalalel	65	830	895	5:15-17
Jared	162	800	962	5:18-20
Enoch	65	300	365	5:21-24
Methuselah	187	782	969	5:25-27
Lamech	182	595	777	5:28-31
Noah 600 at beginning of flood			950	7:11; 9:29
Shem 98 at end of flood			600	11:10-11
Shem	100	500	600	11:10-11
Arpachshad	35	403	438	11:12-13
Shelah	30	403	433	11:14-15
Eber	34	430	464	11:16-17
Peleg	30	209	239	11:18-19
Reu	32	207	239	11:20-21
Serug	30	200	230	11:22-23
Nahor	29	119	148	11:24-25
Terah+	70	135	205	11:26-32

*The author does not mean to imply that these genealogies represent consecutive life spans.
+Terah was the father of Abraham, Nahor, and Haran.

Time Periods of the Flood

DATE	NUMBER OF DAYS	EVENT	GENESIS REFERENCE
Month 2 Day 10	Waited 7	Entered the ark.	7:4, 10
*Month 2 Day 17	Lasted 40	Rain began.	7:4-6, 11, 12
Month 3 Day 26	End of 40	Rain stopped.	7:4, 11
*Month 7 Day 17	End of 150	Ark rested on Ararat.	7:24; 8:4
*Month 10 Day 1	Waited 40	Tops of mountains visible.	8:5-6
Month 11 Day 10	Waited 1	Raven sent.	8:7
Month 11 Day 11	Waited 7	Dove sent; returns.	8:8-9
Month 11 Day 19	Waited 7	Dove sent; returns with olive leaf.	8:10-11
Month 11 Day 27		Dove sent; does not return.	8:12
Month 12 Day 17	End of 150	Water fully receded.	8:3
*Month 1 Day 1		Covering of ark removed.	8:13
*Month 2 Day 27		Earth dry; left ark.	8:14-19

Rows grouped under side labels: "Water prevailed 150 days (7:24)" spans the rain-began through Ark-rested rows; "Water receded 150 days (8:3)" spans the tops-of-mountains through water-fully-receded rows; "Drying of earth" spans the last two rows.

Statistics

One month equals 30 days.
Total time elapsed in the ark = 1 year, 17 days = 360 + 17 = 377 days

7 days waiting + 150 days + 150 days + 70 days = 377 days
            water prevaling   water receding earth drying

*Date notation specifically mentioned in Scripture. (All others are derived.)

Chronology of the Patriarchs

EVENT	AGE	DATE	GENESIS REFERENCE	AGE	DATE	GENESIS REFERENCE
ABRAHAM 2166-1991						
Entrance into Canaan	75	2091	12:4			
Ishmael born	86	2080	16:3			
Isaac born	100	2066	21:5	ISAAC 2066-1886		
Mt. Moriah (?)	115	2051	22	15	2051	22
Isaac marries Rebekah	140	2026	25:20	40	2026	25:20
JACOB 2006-1859				60	2006	25:26
Abraham dies	15	1991	25:7	75	1991	25:7
Jacob goes to Haran	77	1929	28:5	137	1929	28:5
Jacob marries Leah and Rachel	84	1922	29:21-30 30:1, 22-26	144	1922	29:21-30 30:1, 22-26
Joseph born	91	1915	30:25 31:38-41	JOSEPH 1915-1805		
Jacob & family move to Canaan	97	1909	31:17-21	6	1909	31:17-21
Joseph sold into slavery	108	1898	37:2-36	17	1898	37:2-36
Isaac dies	120	1886	35:28-29	29	1886	35:28-29
Joseph given high position	121	1885	41:39-40	30	1885	41:39-40
Jacob and family move to Egypt	130	1876	45:6 47:9	39	1876	45:6 47:9
Jacob dies	147	1859	47:28	56	1859	47:28
Joseph dies	—	—	—	110	1805	50:26

Note: This particular chronological framework with the early dates is presented here as representative of the clear reading of the Masoretic text. Any of the other frameworks can be derived from this.

Patriarchal Family Tree

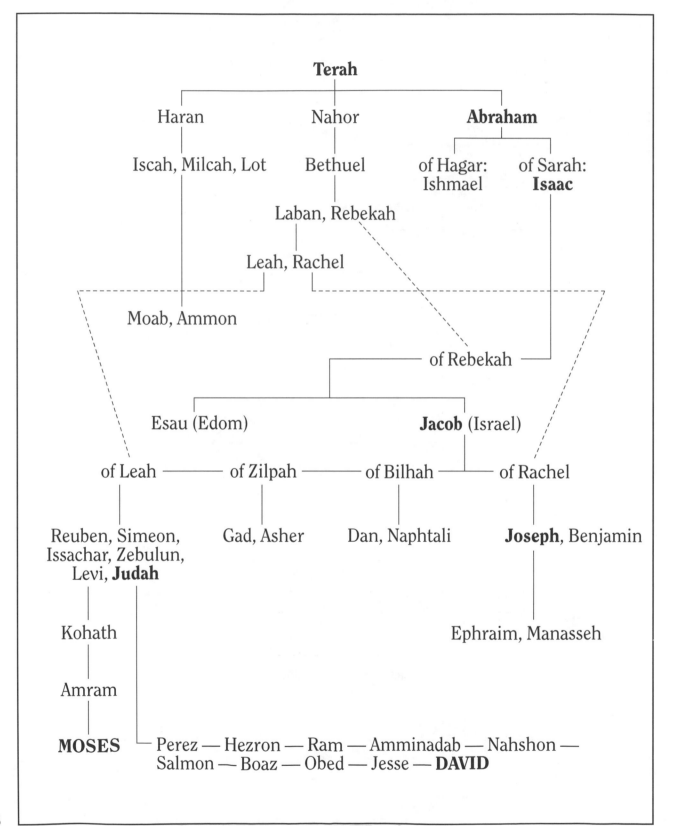

Terah

Haran   Nahor   **Abraham**

Iscah, Milcah, Lot Bethuel of Hagar: of Sarah:
         Ishmael **Isaac**

Laban, Rebekah

Leah, Rachel

Moab, Ammon

of Rebekah

Esau (Edom)   **Jacob** (Israel)

of Leah ——— of Zilpah ——— of Bilhah ——— of Rachel

Reuben, Simeon, Gad, Asher Dan, Naphtali **Joseph**, Benjamin
Issachar, Zebulun,
Levi, **Judah**

Kohath   Ephraim, Manasseh

Amram

MOSES Perez — Hezron — Ram — Amminadab — Nahshon —
     Salmon — Boaz — Obed — Jesse — **DAVID**

Theophanies in Genesis

"I AM YAHWEH"	"I AM EL SHADDAI"
Initiation of agreement	Initiation of fulfillment
ABRAHAM	
Genesis 15:7-17 1. *Occasion:* Ratification of covenant 2. *Emphasis:* Giving of land	Genesis 17:1-8 1. *Occasion:* Indication of acceptance of covenant (circumcision) 2. Accepts name change; Isaac promised within year 3. *Emphasis:* Many descendants, nations, kings will come from you
JACOB	
Genesis 28:13-15 1. *Occasion:* First promise of covenant blessings to Jacob 2. *Emphasis:* Bringing him back to land and giving it to him	Genesis 35:10-12 1. *Occasion:* Indication of acceptance of covenant (destruction of foreign gods, pillar set up) 2. Accepts name change 3. *Emphasis:* Many descendants, nations, kings will come from you

Sons of Jacob

MOTHER	SON	MEANING OF NAME	REFERENCE OF BIRTH (GENESIS)	ORDER OF BLESSING	SYMBOL OF BLESSING	REFERENCE OF BLESSING (GENESIS)
LEAH	Reuben	Behold, a son	29:32	1	Reckless	49:3-4
	Simeon	Hearing	29:33	2	Violence	49:5-7
	Levi	Attachment	29:34	3	Violence	49:5-7
	Judah	Praise	29:35	4	Lion	49:8-12
BILHAH	Dan	Judgment	30:6	7	Serpent	49:16-18
	Naphtali	Wrestle	30:8	10	Doe	49:21
ZILPAH	Gad	Good fortune	30:11	8	Raider	49:19
	Asher	Happy	30:13	9	Rich food	49:20
LEAH	Issachar	Reward	30:18	6	Donkey	49:14-15
	Zebulun	Abode	30:20	5	Ships	49:13
RACHEL	Joseph	May he add	30:24	11	Fruitful	49:22-26
	Benjamin	Son of the right hand	35:18	12	Wolf	49:27

Jewish Calendar

RELI-GIOUS YEAR	CIVIL YEAR	HEBREW MONTH	WESTERN CORRELATION	FARM SEASONS	CLI-MATE	SPECIAL DAYS
1	7	Nisan	March-April	Barley harvest	Latter Rains (Mal-qosh)	14 — Passover 21 — First Fruits
2	8	Iyyar	April-May	General harvest		
3	9	Sivan	May-June	Wheat harvest Vine tending	DRY SEASON	6 — Pentecost
4	10	Tammuz	June-July	First grapes		
5	11	Ab	July-August	Grapes, figs, olives		9 — Destruction of Temple
6	12	Elul	August-September	Vintage		
7	1	Tishri	September-October	Ploughing		1 — New Year 10 — Day of Atonement 15-21 — Feast of Tabernacles
8	2	Marchesvan	October-November	Grain planting	Early Rains (Yoreh) Rain Season	
9	3	Kislev	November-December			25 — Dedication
10	4	Tebet	December-January	Spring growth		
11	5	Shebat	January-February	Winter figs		
12	6	Adar	February-March	Pulling flax Almonds bloom		13-14 — Purim
		Adar Sheni	Intercalary Month			

Jewish Special Days

SPECIAL DAYS	HEBREW NAME	DAY	REFERENCE	READING (MEGILLOTH)	COMMEMORATION
Passover (Feast of Unleavened Bread)	Pesach	14 Nisan	Exod. 12 (Lev. 23:4-8)	Song of Solomon	Deliverance from Egypt
Pentecost	Shavuoth	6 Sivan	Deut. 16:9-12 (Lev. 23:9-14)	Ruth	Celebration of the harvest
9th of Ab	Tish'ah be'ab	9 Ab	No direct reference	Lamentations	Destruction of temple 586 B.C., A.D. 70
Day of Atonement	Yom Kippur	10 Tishri	Lev. 16 (23:26-32)		Sacrifices for sins of the nation
Feast of Tabernacles	Succoth	15-21 Tishri	Neh. 8 (Lev. 23:33-36)	Ecclesiastes	Wanderings in the wilderness
Dedication	Chanukah	25 Kislev	John 10:22		Restoration of temple in 164 B.C.
Lots	Purim	13-14 Adar	Esth. 9	Esther	Failure of plot against Jews by Haman

Laws of the Old Testament

	EXODUS	LEVITICUS	NUMBERS	DEUT
Whom to worship	20:3, 23, 22:20, 23:13, 24, 34:13-17	19:4; 20:2		5:7; 13:1-18
How to treat God				
Sacrifices	20:24-26; 22:29-30; 23:18-19; 29:10-41; 34:19-20, 25-26	chs 1-7; 17; 19:4-8; 20:21-22; 22:18-30	15:2-31; 28:2-8	12:13-14; 17:1
Holy Days	20:8-11; 23:12; 23:14-17; 1:13-17; 34:18, 21-24; 35:2-3	16:1-34; 19:3b, 30; 23:3-34; 26:2	9:10-14; 28:9-29:38	5:13-15; 16:1-17
Vows		ch 27	6:2-21; 30:2-15	23:18, 21-23
Temple ritual	27:20-21; 30:7-10, 19-21	10:9; 24:2-9		
Purity issues and ritual		19:19; 21:1-22:16	5:6-31; 15:38-40; 19:1-22	21:1-9; 22:11-12; 23:1-3
Tithes and offerings	30:12-16		18:8-32	12:17-19; 14:22-29; 15:19-23; 18:1-5; 26:1-15
Sabbatical years		25:8-34		15:1-18
Idolatry	20:4-6	26:1		5:8-10; 7:25-26; 12:2-4; 16:21-22
Blasphemy and Curses	20:7; 22:28	24:14-16		5:11
Social Structure and Ethics				
Leaders				17:14-20
Family	20:12, 14; 21:15, 17; 22:16-17	19:3a, 29, 32; 20:9	27:7-11	5:16, 18; 21:10-21; 22:13-30; 23:17; 24:1-4; 25:5-12
Slaves	21:1-11	19:20; 25:39-55		23:15-16
Land ownership and use	23:10-11	19:9-10; 25:1-7	36:7-9	19:14; 22:9
Personal property	20:15, 17; 21:33-36; 22:1-15	19:11		5:19, 21; 22:1-4; 23:24-25
Respect of person	20:13; 21:12-14, 16, 18-32	19:17-18; 24:17-22		5:17; 24:7
Justice	20:16; 22:21–22, 25-26; 23:1-9	19:11 16, 33 36; 25:35 37	35:11 34	5:20; 16:18-20; 17:2-13; 19:4-13, 15 21; 21:22 23; 22:6 8, 10; 23:19-20; 24:6, 10-22; 25:1-4, 13-15
Sexual and Bodily Purity	22:19	chs 12-15; 18; 20:10-21	5:2-3	22:5; 23:9-14
Warfare				20:1-20; 24:5
Divination	22:18	19:26-28, 31; 20:27		18:9-14
Food Laws	22:31	11:1-47; 20:25		12:15-16, 20-27; 14:3-21

Sacrificial System

NAME	PORTION BURNT	OTHER PORTIONS	ANIMALS	OCCASION OR REASON	REFERENCE
Burnt Offering	All	None	Male without blemish; animal according to wealth	Propitiation for general sin; demonstrates dedication	Lev. 1
Meal Offering or Tribute Offering	Token portion	Eaten by priest	Unleavened cakes or grains, must be salted	General thankfulness for first fruits	Lev. 2
Peace Offering a. Thank Offering b. Vow Offering c. Freewill Offering	Fat portions	Shared in fellowship meal by priest and offerer	Male or female without blemish according to wealth; freewill: slight blemish allowed	Fellowship a. For an unexpected blessing b. For deliverance when a vow was made on that condition c. For general thankfulness	Lev. 3 Lev. 22:18-30
Sin Offering	Fat portions	Eaten by priest	Priest or congregation: bull king: he-goat individual: she-goat	Applies basically to situation where purification is needed	Lev. 4
Guilt Offering	Fat portions	Eaten by priest	Ram without blemish	Applies to situation where there has been desecration or de-sacrilization of something holy or where there is objective guilt	Lev. 5-6:7

Clean and Unclean Animals

CLASSES	CLEAN	UNCLEAN
Mammals	Two qualifications: 1. Cloven hoofs 2. Chewing of the cud Lev. 11:3-7 Deut. 14:6-8	Carnivores and those not meeting both "clean" qualifications
Birds	Those not specifically listed as forbidden	Birds of prey or scavengers Lev. 11:13-19 Deut. 14:11-20
Reptiles	None	All Lev. 11:29-30
Water Animals	Two qualifications: 1. Fins 2. Scales Lev. 11:9-12 Deut. 14:9-10	Those not meeting both "clean" qualifications
Insects	Those in the grasshopper family Lev. 11:20-23	Winged quadrupeds

Basic Reasons:

1. Holiness demanded being like God. Many restrictions to Israelite diet are derived from restrictions to Yahweh's "diet" (i.e., animals that were unacceptable for sacrifice).
2. Unclean animals fail to conform in some way to the expectations of the group to which they belong.
3. Some animals were considered unclean because of their association with pagan cults.

The Decalogue and Deuteronomy

DIVINE	MAIN ISSUES	HUMAN
1 Ex. 20:2-3 Deut. 5:6,7 God should be our top priority and final authority. We owe Him preference and obedience. Deut. 6-11	**Authority**	**5** Ex. 20:12 Deut. 5:16 Human authority must not sidetrack God's authority. Deut. 16:18-18:22
2 Ex. 20:4-6 Deut. 5:8-10 Worship must reflect a proper view of God. It cannot be manipulative or self-serving. It cannot accommodate to the world's standards. Deut. 12	**Dignity**	**6 7 8** Ex. 20:13-14-15 Deut. 5:17-18-19 The dignity of man must be preserved—involves his life, his family and his status. Deut. 19:1-21:23 Deut. 22:1-23:14 Deut. 23:15-24:7
3 Ex. 20:7 Deut. 5:11 Must take our commitment to God seriously by remaining above reproach and avoiding anything that will lead astray. Deut. 13:1-14:21	**Commitment**	**9** Ex. 20:16 Deut. 5:20 Must take our commitments to fellow man seriously. Deut. 24:8-24:16
4 Ex. 20:8-11 Deut. 5:12-15 God has a right to our gratitude shown by dedicating things to Him; and a right to ask compassion in His name. Deut. 14:22-16:17	**Rights and Privileges**	**10** Ex. 20:17 Deut. 5:21 Must understand the limits to our rights and must not violate the rights of others. Deut. 24:17-26:15

Note: For fuller discussion of the relationship between the laws of Deuteronomy and the Decalogue, see Hill and Walton, *A Survey of the Old Testament.*

Parallels Between the Law and Wisdom

LAW AND WISDOM BOTH HAVE SECULAR FUNCTIONS
OUTSIDE OF ISRAEL, BUT ARE TRANSFORMED
INTO SPIRITUAL CONCEPTS IN ISRAEL
BY GOD'S REVEALED RELATIONSHIP TO THEM.

	LAW	WISDOM
SPIRITUAL FOUNDATION God is source	"You shall be holy, for I, the Lord your God am holy" (Lev. 19:2)	"The fear of the Lord is the beginning of wisdom" (Prov. 9:10)
MOTIVATION Only a God-centered perspective gives ultimate value	Not just so society runs smoothly, rather so that we do what is right	Not pursued for personal fulfillment, rather so that we become people of faith
FOCUS OF GOD'S SELF-REVELATION	God is characterized by absolute morality	God is characterized by unfathomable wisdom

Chronology of the Judges
Joshua and the Elders—1406–1385

OPPRESSOR	KING	YEARS	ESTIMATED DATES B.C.	REFERENCE (ALL JUDGES)	JUDGE	TRIBE	YEARS	PLACE OF BATTLE
Mesopotamia	Cushan-rishathaim	8	1385-1377	3:8				
			1377-1337	3:9-11	Othniel	Judah	40	
Moabites	Eglon	18	1337-1319	3:12-14				
			1319-1239	3:15-30	Ehud	Benjamin	80	Jericho
Philistines				3:31				
				3:31	Shamgar			
Canaanites	Jabin	20	1259-1239	4:2-3				
			1239-1199	4:4-5:31	Deborah	Ephraim	40	Esdraelon
Midianites	Oreb, Zeeb, Zebah, Zalmunna	7	1199-1192	6:1-6				
			1192-1152	6:7-8:35	Gideon	Manasseh	40	Hill of Moreh
Civil war of Abimelech			1152-1149	9	killed at Thebez			
			1149-1126	10:1-2	Tola	Issachar	23	
			1126-1104	10:3-6	Jair	Gilead	22	
Ammonites		18	1104-1086	10:7-9				
			1086-1080	10:10-12:7	Jephthah	Gilead	6	Transjordan
			1080-1072	12:8-10	Ibzan	Judah	8	
			1072-1062	12:11-12	Elon	Zebulun	10	
			1062-1055	12:13-15	Abdon	Ephraim	7	
Philistines		40	1115-1075	13:1				
			1075-1055	13:2-16:31	Samson	Dan	20	

26

The chronology of the judges is very uncertain because we are not told where overlapping occurs. This is one possible alignment.

Correlation of Samuel/Kings and Chronicles

SAMUEL/KINGS	TOPICS	CHRONICLES
	Genealogies	1 Chr 1-9
1 Sam 1-3, 7	Samuel	
1 Sam 4-6	Capture of ark	
1 Sam 8-15	Saul	1 Chr 10
1 Sam 16-31	David's youth	
2 Sam 1-10	David's successes	1 Chr 11:1-9; 13-20
2 Sam 11-12	David and Bathsheba	
2 Sam 13-21	David's troubles	
2 Sam 22-23	Misc. David	1 Chr 11:10-12:40; 22-29
2 Sam 24	David's census	1 Chr 21
1 Kgs 1-3	Solomon's wisdom	2 Chr 1
1 Kgs 5-9:9	Temple	2 Chr 2-7
1 Kgs 4, 9-10	Misc. Solomon	2 Chr 8-9
1 Kgs 11	Solomon's troubles	
1 Kgs 12:1-24; 14:21-31	Rehoboam	2 Chr 10-12
1 Kgs 11:26-40; 12:25-14:20	*Jeroboam*	
1 Kgs 15:1-8	Abijam	2 Chr 13
1 Kgs 15:9-24	Asa	2 Chr 14-16
1 Kgs 15:25-31	*Nadab*	
1 Kgs 15:27-28; 16:1-7	*Baasha*	
1 Kgs 16:8-14	*Elah*	
1 Kgs 16:9-20	*Zimri*	
1 Kgs 16:21-28	*Omri*	
1 Kgs 16:29-34; 20-22:40	*Ahab*	
1 Kgs 17-19	Elijah	
1 Kgs 22:41-50	Jehoshaphat	2 Chr 17-20
1 Kgs 22:51-53; 2 Kgs 1:1-18	*Ahaziah*	
2 Kgs 2-8:15	Elisha	
2 Kgs 8:16-24	Jehoram	2 Chr 21
2 Kgs 3:1-3; 9:14-24	*Jehoram*	

SAMUEL/KINGS	TOPICS	CHRONICLES
2 Kgs 8:25-29; 9, 21-28	Ahaziah	2 Chr 22:1-9
2 Kgs 9-10	*Jehu*	
2 Kgs 11	Athaliah	2 Chr 22:10-23:21
2 Kgs 12	Joash	2 Chr 24
2 Kgs 13:1-9	*Jehoahaz*	
2 Kgs 13:10-25; 14:8-16	*Jehoash*	
2 Kgs 14:1-22	Amaziah	2 Chr 25
2 Kgs 14:23-29	*Jeroboam II*	
2 Kgs 15:1-7	Uzziah (Azariah)	2 Chr 26
2 Kgs 15:8-12	*Zechariah*	
2 Kgs 15:13-15	*Shallum*	
2 Kgs 15:16-22	*Menahem*	
2 Kgs 15:32-38	Jotham	2 Chr 27
2 Kgs 15:23-26	*Pekahiah*	
2 Kgs 15:27-31	*Pekah*	
2 Kgs 16	Ahaz	2 Chr 28
2 Kgs 17:1-5	*Hoshea*	
2 Kgs 17:7-41	Fall of Samaria	
2 Kgs 18-20	Hezekiah	2 Chr 29-32
2 Kgs 21:1-18	Manasseh	2 Chr 33:1-20
2 Kgs 21:19-26	Amon	2 Chr 33:21-25
2 Kgs 22-23:30	Josiah	2 Chr 34-35
2 Kgs 23:31-34	Jehoahaz	2 Chr 36:1-3
2 Kgs 24:1-7	Jehoiakim	2 Chr 36:4-8
2 Kgs 24:8-17	Jehoiachin	2 Chr 36:9-10
2 Kgs 24:18-20	Zedekiah	2 Chr 36:11-14
2 Kgs 25:1-21	Fall of Jerusalem	2 Chr 36:15-21
2 Kgs 25:22-26	Gedaliah	
2 Kgs 25:27-30	Jehoiachin's exile	
	Cyrus' decree	2 Chr 36:22-23

Note: Kings of the northern kingdom of Israel are given in italics.

27

Family and Ancestry of David

ANCESTRY (Ruth 4:18-22; 1 Chron. 2:1-15)	
Patriarchs	Abraham – Isaac – Jacob – Judah
Egypt	Perez – Hezron – Ram Amminadab – Nahshon
Conquest and Judges	Salmon – Boaz – Obed – Jesse – David

FAMILY (2 Sam. 3:2-5; 5:14-16; 1 Chron. 3:5-8)		
Children of Jesse	Wives of David	Sons of David
Sons: Eliab	Ahinoam	Amnon (killed by Absalom)
Abinadab	Abigail	Chileab (died in youth)
Shammah	Maacah	Absalom (killed by Joab)
Nethanel	Haggith	Adonijah (deposed by Solomon)
Raddai	Abital	Shephatiah
Ozem	Eglah	Ithream
David	Bathsheba	Solomon, Shimea, Shobab, Nathan
Daughters: Zeruiah (mother of Joab, Abishai, Asahel)	Michal	None
Abigail (mother of Amasa)	Various concubines	Ibhar, Elishama, Eliphelet, Nogah, Nepheg, Japhia, Eliada, Elishama, Eliphelet

Narrative Emphasis
in the History of the United Monarchy

	SAUL	DAVID	SOLOMON
APPOINTMENT	1. By Samuel 2. Public process 3. Activated by the Spirit	1. By Samuel 2. Long process 3. By people	1. By David 2. By Zadok and Nathan
SUCCESSES AND POTENTIAL	Victory over Ammonites	1. Taking of Jerusalem 2. Defeat of Philistines 3. Bringing ark back 4. Covenant 5. Expansion of empire	1. Dream and request for wisdom 2. Wisdom and administration of empire 3. Building of temple
FAILURES	1. Impatient offering 2. Placing people under improper oath 3. Disobeying instructions in Amalekite war	1. Adultery with Bathsheba and murder of Uriah 2. Wrongful taking of census	1. Foreign wives' religious practices accommodated 2. Labor and tax on people
RESULTS OF FAILURES	Bad judgment, incompetence, and jealousy	1. Bloodshed within family (Amnon, Absalom, Adonijah) 2. Rebellion in kingdom (Absalom, Sheba)	1. Military problems 2. Division of kingdom

The Kings of Judah
(Southern Kingdom)

	HAYES AND HOOKER	THIELE	BRIGHT	COGAN AND TADMOR
REHOBOAM	926-910	931-913	922-915	928-911
ABIJAH	909-907	931-911	915-913	911-908
ASA	906-878 (866)	911-870	913-873	908-867
JEHOSHAPHAT	877-853	872-848	873-849	870-846
JEHORAM	852-841	853-841	849-843	851-843
AHAZIAH	840	841	843/2	843-842
ATHALIAH	839-833	841-835	842-837	842-836
JOASH (Jehoash)	832-803 (793)	835-796	837-800	836-798
AMAZIAH	802-786 (774)	796-767	800-783	798-769
AZARIAH (Uzziah)	785-760 (734)	792-740	783-742	785-733
JOTHAM	759-744	750-732	750-735	758-743
AHAZ	743-728	735-716	735-715	743-727
HEZEKIAH	727-699	716-687	715-687/6	727-698
MANASSEH	698-644	697-643	687/6-642	698-642
AMON	643-642	643-641	642-640	641-640
JOSIAH	641-610	641-609	640-609	639-609
JEHOAHAZ	3 months	609	609	609
JEHOIAKIM	608-598	609-598	609-598	608-598
JEHOIACHIN	3 months	598-597	598/7	597
ZEDEKIAH	596-586	597-586	597-587	596-586

Chronologies for the Hebrew monarchies will vary between one and ten years depending on the source consulted. The sources cited are J. H. Hayes and P. K. Hooker, *A New Chronology for the Kings of Israel and Judah* (Atlanta: John Knox, 1988); E. R. Thiele, *The Mysterious Numbers of the Hebrew Kings,* rev. ed. (Grand Rapids: Zondervan, 1983); J. Bright, *A History of Israel,* 3d ed. (Philadel-

The Kings of Israel
(Northern Kingdom)

	HAYES AND HOOKER	THIELE	BRIGHT	COGAN AND TADMOR
JEROBOAM	927-906	931-910	922-901	928-907
NADAB	905-904	910-909	901-900	907-906
BAASHA	903-882 (880)	909-886	900-877	906-883
ELAH	881-880	886-885	877-876	883-882
ZIMRI	7 days	885	876	882
OMRI	879-869	885-874	876-869	882-871
AHAB	868-854	874-853	869-850	873-852
AHAZIAH	853-852	853-852	850-849	852-851
JEHORAM (Joram)	851-840	852-841	849-843/2	851-842
JEHU	839-822	841-814	843/2-815	842-814
JEHOAHAZ	821-805	814-798	815-802	817-800
JEHOASH (Joash)	804-789	798-782	802-786	800-784
JEROBOAM II	788-748	793-753	786-746	789-748
ZECHARIAH	6 months	753-752	746-745	748-747
SHALLUM	1 month	752	745	747
MENAHEM	746-737	752-742	745-737	747-737
PEKAHIAH	736-735	742-740	737-736	737-735
PEKAH	734-731	752-732	736-732	735-732
HOSHEA	730-722	732-722	732-724	732-724

phia: Westminster, 1981); and M. Cogan and H. Tadmor, *Second Kings,* in AB, vol. 11 (Garden City, N.Y.: Doubleday, 1988). In addition, see J. Finegan, *Handbook of Biblical Chronology* (Princeton: Princeton Univ. Press, 1964); and W. R. Wifall, "The Chronology of the Divided Monarchy of Israel," *Zeitschrift für die Alttestamentliche Wissenschaft* 80 (1968): 319–37.

The Dynasties of the Northern Kingdom

KING	HOW ACCESSION WAS GAINED	FATHER
I. DYNASTY OF JEROBOAM		
Jeroboam	Chosen by the people	Nebat
Nadab	Inherited	Jeroboam
II. DYNASTY OF BAASHA		
Baasha	Assassination	Common
Elah	Inherited	Baasha
III. DYNASTY OF ZIMRI		
Zimri	Assassination	Common
IV. DYNASTY OF OMRI		
Omri	Declared so by army	Common
Ahab	Inherited	Omri
Ahaziah	Inherited	Ahab
Jehoram	Inherited	Ahab
V. DYNASTY OF JEHU		
Jehu	Assassination	Nimshi
Jehoahaz	Inherited	Jehu
Jehoash	Inherited	Jehoahaz
Jeroboam II	Inherited	Jehoash
Zechariah	Inherited	Jeroboam II
VI. DYNASTY OF SHALLUM		
Shallum	Assassination	Jabesh
VII. DYNASTY OF MENAHEM		
Menahem	Assassination	Gadi
Pekahiah	Inherited	Menahem
VIII. DYNASTY OF PEKAH		
Pekah	Coup d'état	Remaliah
IX. DYNASTY OF HOSHEA		
Hoshea	Assassination	Elah

Succession and Intermarriage Among the 9th c. Royal Houses of Israel and Judah

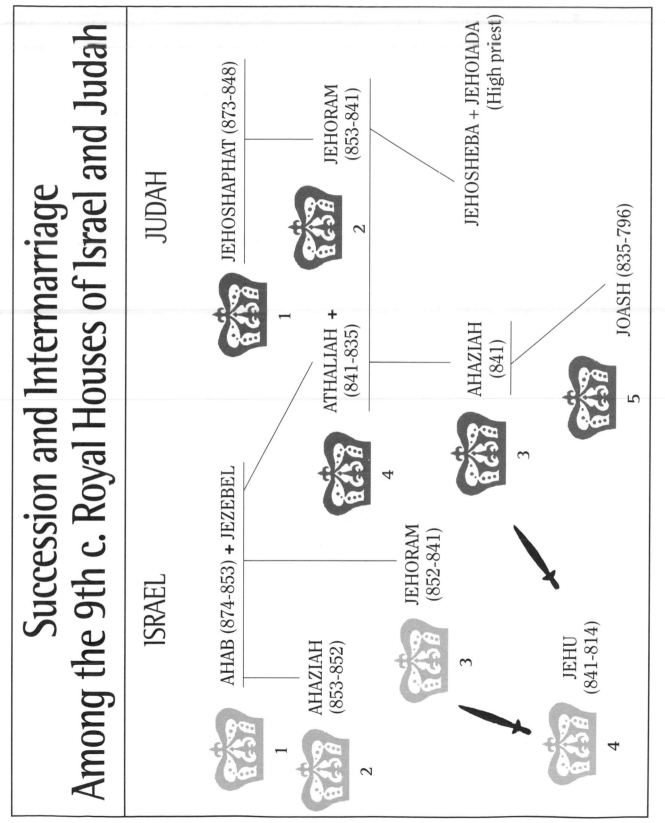

ISRAEL

JUDAH

AHAB (874-853) + JEZEBEL

JEHOSHAPHAT (873-848)

AHAZIAH (853-852) — 1

JEHORAM (852-841) — 3

ATHALIAH + (841-835) — 4

JEHORAM (853-841) — 2

JEHOSHEBA + JEHOIADA (High priest)

AHAZIAH (841) — 3

JOASH (835-796) — 5

JEHU (841-814) — 4

33

Source Books
Mentioned in Scripture

	SOURCE BOOK	REFERENCE
POETIC	Book of the Wars of the Lord	Num. 21:14
	Book of Yashar (the Upright)	Josh. 10:13; 2 Sam. 1:18
ROYAL COURT RECORDS	The Records of the Chronicles of King David	1 Chron. 27:24
	The Book of the Kings of Israel and Judah The Book of the Kings of Judah and Israel	2 Chron. 27:7; 35:27; 36:8 2 Chron. 16:11; 25:26; 28:26; 32:32
	The Book of the Kings of Israel	1 Chron. 9:1; 2 Chron. 20:34
	The Commentary on the Book of Kings	2 Chron. 24:27
	The Words of the Kings of Israel	2 Chron. 33:18
	The Decree of David the King of Israel and the Decree of Solomon his son	2 Chron. 35:4
RECORDS BY PROPHETS	The Words of Samuel the Seer	1 Chron. 29:29
	The Words of Nathan the Prophet	1 Chron. 29:29; 2 Chron. 9:29
	The Words of Gad the Seer	1 Chron. 29:29
	The Prophecy of Ahijah the Shilonite	2 Chron. 9:29
	The Visions of Iddo the Seer	2 Chron. 9:29; 12:15; 13:22
	The Words of Shemaiah the Prophet	2 Chron. 12:15
	The Words of Jehu the son of Hanani	2 Chron. 20:34
	The Deeds of Uzziah by Isaiah the Prophet	2 Chron. 26:22; 32:32
	The Chronicles of Hozai (Seers)	2 Chron. 33:19

Returns From Exile

RETURN	FIRST	SECOND	THIRD
Reference	Ezra 1-6	Ezra 7-10	Nehemiah 1-13
Date	538 B.C.	458 B.C	444 B.C.
Leaders	Sheshbazzar Zerubbabel Jeshua	Ezra	Nehemiah
Persian King	Cyrus	Artaxerxes Longimanus	Artaxerxes Longimanus
Elements of the Decree	As many as wished to could return. Temple could be rebuilt, partially financed by royal treasury. Vessels returned.	As many as wished to could return. Finances provided by royal treasury. Allowed to have own civil magistrates.	Allowed to rebuild the wall
Number Returning	42,360 7,337 (servants) 49,697	1,500 men 38 Levites 220 helpers 1,758	Unknown
Events, Accomplishments, and Problems	Temple begun; sacrifices made and Feast of Tabernacles celebrated. Samaritans made trouble, and work ceased until 520. Temple completed in 516.	Problems with intermarriage	Wall rebuilt in 52 days, despite opposition from Sanballat, Tobiah, and Geshem. Walls dedicated and Law read.

Chronological Sequence in the Book of Ezra

CYRUS 539–530	CAMBYSES 530–522	DARIUS 522–486	XERXES 486–464	ARTAXERXES 464–424

538 Temple project begun

536 Work on temple stopped

520 Work on Temple resumed by Zerubbabel & Joshua, encouraged by Haggai & Zechariah

515 Temple com-pleted

530   520   510   500   490   480   470   460

Ezra 1–4:5,24	Ezra 5–6		Ezra 4:6 False accusations filed	Ezra 4:7–23	Ezra 7–10

Battles in the Wilderness
1446–1406 B.C.

Opponent	Place of Battle	King	Aggressor	Victor	Scripture
Amalek	Rephidim		Amalek	Israel	Exod. 17:8-16
Amalek and Canaanites	Hormah		Israel	Amalek	Num. 14:45
Arad	Hormah		Arad	Israel	Num. 21:1-3
Amorites	Jahaz	Sihon	Amorites	Israel	Num. 21:21-25
Bashan	Edrei	Og	Israel	Israel	Num. 21:33-35
Midian		Evi, Rekem, Zur, Hur, Reba	Israel	Israel	Num. 31:1-12

Battles of Joshua's Conquest

SECURING THE CENTRAL CORRIDOR		
OPPONENT	BATTLE SITE	JOSHUA REFERENCE
Jericho	Jericho	6:12-27
Ai	Ai	7:2-6
Ai and Bethel	Ai	8:1-29

THE SOUTHERN COALITION		
Coalition of Amorites led by Adoni-Zedek of Jerusalem and including Hebron, Jarmuth, Lachish, and Eglon	Initial encounter at Gibeon with pursuit through Beth-Horon and the Valley of Aijalon ending at Azekah	10:1-27

Follow-up sieges at Makkedah, Libnah, Lachish, Gezer, Eglon, Hebron, and Debir (10:28-39)

THE NORTHERN COALITION		
Coalition led by Jabin of Hazor and including many cities of the north	Initial encounter by the Waters of Merom with pursuit west to Sidon and Misrephoth-maim and the Mizpeh Valley to the NE	11:1-9

Follow-up sieges at Hazor and other royal cities unnamed (11:10-15)

Battles of the Judges Period

OPPONENT	KING	ISRAEL'S DELIVERER	VICTOR	LOCATION OF BATTLE	SCRIPTURE (ALL IN JUDGES)
Bezek	Adoni-bezek	—	Judah	Bezek	1:4-7
Kiriath-Arba (Hebron)	Sheshai, Ahiman, Talmai	**Caleb**	Judah	Hebron	1:10
Kiriath-Sepher (Debir)	—	**Othniel**	Judah	Debir	1:12-13
Various cities	—	—	Judah	Various cities	1:17-18
Luz (Bethel)	—	—	Manasseh, Ephraim	Bethel	1:22-25
Mesopotamia	Cushan-rishathaim	**Othniel**	Israel	—	3:10
Moab	Eglon	**Ehud**	Israel	Jericho	3:15-30
Hazor	Jabin	**Deborah**	Israel	Esdraelon	4:4-16
Midianites	Zeeb, Zebah, Oreb, Zalmunna	**Gideon**	Israel	Hill of Moreh	7:7-8:25
Civil: Abimelek vs. Shechem	Abimelek	**Gaal**	Abimelek	Shechem	9:34-41
Civil: Abimelek vs. Thebez	Abimelek	—	Israel	Thebez	9:50-57
Ammonites	—	**Jephthah**	Israel	Transjordan	11:29-33
Civil: Gileadites vs. Ephraimites	—	**Jephthah**	Gilead	Zaphon	12:1-6
Laish	—	—	Dan	Laish	18:27-29
Civil: Israel vs. Benjaminites	—	—	Israel	Gibeah	20:1-48

Wars of Saul
1050–1010 B.C.

OPPONENT	KING OR CHAMPION	PLACE OF BATTLE	AGGRESSOR	VICTOR	REASON FOR BATTLE	SCRIPTURE
Ammonites	Nahash	Jabesh-gilead	Ammon	Israel	To gain control of Jabesh-gilead	1 Sam. 11:1-11
Philistines		Geba	Israel	Israel	To chase Philistines from Israelite territory	1 Sam. 13:3
Philistines		Michmash	Philistia	Israel	To regain foothold in Israel	1 Sam. 13:5-14:46
Moab, Ammon, Edom, Zobah		Various places		Israel	Protection and enlargement of borders	1 Sam. 14:47
Amalekites	Agag	Southwest Palestine	Israel	Israel	Destruction commanded by God	1 Sam. 15:1-9
Philistines	Goliath	Valley of Elah	Philistia	Israel	Conquest of Israel	1 Sam. 17:1-54
Philistines	Achish and others	Mount Gilboa	Philistia	Philistia	Conquest of Israel	1 Sam. 31:1-6

Establishment of the Davidic Empire

OPPONENT	KING	PLACE OF BATTLE	AGGRESSOR	VICTOR	REFERENCE
Internal: regime of Saul	Ishbosheth	Pool of Gibeon	Mutual agreement	David	2 Sam. 2:12-29
Philistines		Valley of Rephaim	Philistines	Israel	2 Sam. 5:17-25
Jebusites		Jerusalem	Israel	Israel	1 Chron. 11:4-7
Moabites			Israel	Israel	2 Sam. 8:2
Zobah and Syria	Hadadezer	Near Euphrates	Israel	Israel	2 Sam. 8:3-6
Edomites		Valley of Salt	Israel	Israel	1 Chron. 18:12
Ammon, Zobah, and Syria	Hanun, Hadadezer	Helam	Israel	Israel	2 Sam. 10:1-19
Ammon	Hanun	Rabbah	Israel	Israel	2 Sam. 12:26-31
Internal: rebellion of Absalom	Absalom	Mahanaim Forest of Ephraim	David	David	2 Sam. 18:1-16
Internal: rebellion of Sheba	Sheba (leader)	Abel-Beth Maacah	David	David	2 Sam. 20:1-22
Philistines		Gob	Philistines	Israel	2 Sam. 21:18-22

Military Conflicts

APPROX. DATE (Thiele)	KING OF ISRAEL	OPPOSING COUNTRY	OPPOSING KING	AGGRESSOR	VICTOR
925	Jeroboam	Syria	Rezon	Syria	Syria
925	Jeroboam	Philistia		Philistia	Philistia
925	Jeroboam	Moab		Moab	Moab
912	Jeroboam	Judah	Abijam	Judah	Judah
909	Nadab	Philistia		Israel	Philistia
895	Baasha	Judah	Asa	Israel	Judah
890	Baasha	Syria	Ben-hadad I	Syria	Syria
885	Zimri	Civil War	Omri	Omri	Omri
881	Omri	Civil War	Tibni	Omri	Omri
877	Omri	Moab		Israel	Israel
853	Ahab	Syria	Ben-hadad I	Syria	Israel
853	Ahab	Syria	Ben-hadad I	Israel	Israel
853	Ahab	Assyria	Shalmaneser III	Assyria	Israel
853	Ahab	Syria	Ben-hadad I	Israel	Syria
850	Jehoram	Moab	Mesha	Moab	Moab
845	Jehoram	Syria	Ben-hadad I	Syria	Israel
845	Jehoram	Syria	Ben-hadad I	Syria	Israel
841	Jehoram	Syria	Hazael	Israel	Syria
820	Jehu	Syria	Hazael	Syria	Syria
810	Jehoahaz	Syria	Hazael	Syria	Syria
798	Jehoash	Syria	Ben-hadad II	Israel	Israel
795	Jehoash	Syria	Ben-hadad II	Israel	Israel
793	Jehoash	Syria	Ben-hadad II	Israel	Israel
790	Jehoash	Judah	Amaziah	Judah	Israel
780	Jeroboam II	Syria	Ben-hadad II	Israel	Israel
735	Pekah	Judah	Ahaz	Israel	Judah
733	Pekah	Assyria	Tiglath-pileser III	Assyria	Assyria
722	Hoshea	Assyria	Shalmaneser V	Assyria	Assyria

# of Israel

PLACE OF BATTLE	TERRITORY GAINED	REASON FOR AGGRESSION	SCRIPTURE
Mt. Zemaraim Gibbethon	Syria Philistia Moab Various cities None	Revolution for freedom Revolution for freedom Revolution for freedom To regain territory To gain back lost territory	2 Chron. 13:2-20 1 Kings 15:27
Ramah Various cities Tirzah	Ramah Naphtali Israel Israel Moab	To gain control of route north In response to Asa's call Take throne To totally control throne Conquest of Moab	1 Kings 15:16-17 { 1 Kings 15:20; 2 Chron. 16:4-5 1 Kings 16:17-18 1 Kings 16:22
Samaria Aphek Qarqar Ramoth-gilead	None None None None Moab	Conquest of Israel To chase from country Conquest of Israel To take back subjugated city Revolution for freedom	1 Kings 20:1-21 1 Kings 20:22-30 { 1 Kings 22:29-37; 2 Chron. 13:28-31 2 Kings 3:4-27
Various cities Samaria Ramoth-gilead Various cities Various cities	None None None Transjordan Various cities	To gain control of territory Conquest of Israel To take back subjugated city To gain control of territory To gain control of country	2 Kings 6:8 2 Kings 6:24-7:8 2 Kings 8:28-29 2 Kings 10:32-33 2 Kings 13:3-7, 22
Various cities Various cities Various cities Beth-shemesh Various cities	Various cities Various cities Various cities None Control of Syria	Recovery of cities Recovery of cities Recovery of cities Show of strength, revenge Conquest of northern territory	2 Kings 13:25 2 Kings 13:25 2 Kings 13:25 2 Kings 13:12; 14:11-13 2 Kings 14:25-28
Jerusalem Various cities Samaria	None Naphtali Israel	To persuade to join alliance against Assyria Subjugation, responding to Ahaz' request Conquest of Israel	{ 2 Kings 15:37; 16:5-6 2 Kings 15:29 2 Kings 17:4-6

Military Conflicts

APPROX. DATE (Thiele)	KING OF JUDAH	OPPOSING COUNTRY	OPPOSING KING	AGRESSOR	VICTOR
925	Rehoboam	Egypt	Sheshonq I	Egypt	Egypt
912	Abijam	Israel	Jeroboam	Judah	Judah
900	Asa	Ethiopia (Egypt)	Zerah	Egypt	Judah
895	Asa	Israel	Baasha	Israel	Judah
853	Jehoshaphat	Syria	Ben-hadad I	Judah	Syria
853	Jehoshaphat	Edom, Moab, Ammon		Edom, Moab, Ammon	Judah
850	Jehoshaphat	Moab		Moab	Moab
845	Joram	Edom		Edom	Edom
845	Joram	Libnah		Libnah	Libnah
842	Joram	Philistia, Arabia		Philistia, Arabia	Philistia, Arabia
841	Ahaziah	Syria	Hazael	Judah	Syria
796	Joash	Syria	Hazael	Syria	Syria
794	Amaziah	Edom		Judah	Judah
790	Amaziah	Israel	Jehoash	Judah	Israel
785	Uzziah	Philistia, Arabia		Judah	Judah
743	Uzziah	Assyria	Tiglath-pileser III	Assyria	Assyria
738	Jotham	Ammon		Judah	Judah
735	Ahaz	Israel, Syria	Pekah, Rezin	Israel, Syria	Judah
735	Ahaz	Edom		Edom	Edom
735	Ahaz	Philistia		Philistia	Philistia
733	Ahaz	Assyria	Tiglath-pileser III	Assyria	Assyria
715	Hezekiah	Philistia		Judah	Judah
701	Hezekiah	Assyria	Sennacherib	Assyria	Judah
650	Manasseh	Assyria	Ashurbanipal	Assyria	Assyria
609	Josiah	Egypt	Necho	Judah	Egypt
607	Jehoiakim	Moab, Syria		Moab, Syria	
605	Jehoiakim	Babylon	Nebuchadnezzar	Babylon	Babylon
597	Jehoiachin	Babylon	Nebuchadnezzar	Babylon	Babylon
586	Zedekiah	Babylon	Nebuchadnezzar	Babylon	Babylon

# of Judah

PLACE OF BATTLE	TERRITORY GAINED	REASON FOR AGGRESSION	SCRIPTURE
Various cities	Various cities	Conquest of Judah	{ 1 Kings 14:25-28; 2 Chron. 12:2-12
Mt. Zemaraim	Various cities	To regain territory	2 Chron. 13:2-20
Mareshah	None	Conquest of Judah	2 Chron. 14:9-15
Ramah	Ramah	To gain control of route north	1 Kings 15:16-17
Ramoth-gilead	None	To take back subjugated city	{ 1 Kings 22:29-37; 2 Chron. 18:28-34
En-gedi	None	Conquest of Judah	2 Chron. 20:1
	Moab	Revolution for freedom from Israel	2 Kings 3:4-27
	Edom	Revolution for freedom from Judah	{ 2 Kings 8:22; 2 Chron. 21:8-10
	Libnah	Revolution for freedom from Judah	{ 2 Kings 8:22; 2 Chron. 21:10
Jerusalem	None	Plundering	2 Chron. 21:16-17
Ramoth-gilead	None	To take back subjugated city	{ 2 Kings 8:28-29; 2 Chron. 22:5-6
Various cities	Various cities	To subjugate cities of Judah	{ 2 Kings 12:18; 2 Chron. 24:23-24
Valley of Salt	Edom	Conquest of Edom	{ 2 Kings 14:7; 2 Chron. 25:11-13
Beth-shemesh	None	Show of strength, revenge to Israel mercenaries	{ 2 Kings 13:12; 14:11-13; 2 Chron. 25:17-24
Various cities	Various cities	Subjugation of cities	2 Chron. 26:6-7
	None in Judah	Conquest of northern territory	not in Scripture
		Subjugation of Ammon	2 Chron. 27:5
Jerusalem	None	To persuade to join alliance against Assyria	{ 2 Kings 15:37; 16:5-6; 2 Chron. 28:5-6
	Edom	Plundering	2 Chron. 28:17
Various cities	Various cities	Plundering	2 Chron. 28:18
	None	Subjugation of territory	2 Chron. 28:20
Various cities	Various cities	Subjugation of Philistia	2 Kings 18:8
Jerusalem	None	Conquest of Judah	{ 2 Kings 18:13-19:27; 2 Chron. 32:1-23
	None	Subjugation of Judah	2 Chron. 33:11
Megiddo	Control of Judah	To stop Egypt from aiding Assyria	{ 2 Kings 23:29; 2 Chron. 35:20-24
Various cities	Various cities	Plundering on command from Babylon	2 Kings 24:2
Jerusalem	None	Subjugation and captives	2 Chron. 36:6
Jerusalem	Judah	Subjugation and captives	{ 2 Kings 24:10-12; 2 Chron. 36:10
		Conquest of Judah	{ 2 Kings 25; 2 Chron. 36:13-21

Major Neo-Assyrian Campaigns in Syro-Palestine

DATE	ASSYRIAN KING	MAJOR TARGETS	RESULTS
877	Ashur-nasirpal II	Tyre—Sidon—Byblos	Collection of tribute
853	Shalmaneser III	Battle of Qarqar against western coalition	Assyrian expansion halted
841	Shalmaneser III	Damascus—Megiddo—Tyre—Sidon	Stele erected on Mt. Carmel Jehu paid tribute
805	Adad-nirari III	Damascus	Damascus captured Joash paid tribute
743-738	Tiglath-pileser III	Campaigned against Urartians in N. Syria	Damascus and Menahem of Israel paid tribute
734	Tiglath-pileser III	Acco—Aphek—Gezer—Gaza—Ashkelon	Ahaz probably paid tribute
733	Tiglath-pileser III	Hazor—Megiddo	Most of northern kingdom of Israel annexed
732	Tiglath-pileser III	Damascus	Samaria submits Hoshea placed on throne
724-722	Shalmaneser V	Tyre—Shechem—Samaria	Fall of Samaria Remainder of Israel annexed
720	Sargon II	Hamath—Philistia—Tyre	Hamath, Gaza, and Tyre conquered Judah and Egypt paid tribute
712	Sargon II	Damascus—Beth-shan—Megiddo—Ashdod	Ashdod annexed Hezekiah paid tribute
701	Sennacherib	Tyre—Ekron—Gath—Lachish—Jerusalem	Slaughter of Assyrians outside Jerusalem

Note: Shalmaneser III also campaigned in the west in 849, 848, and 845, but there is little information on these campaigns in the sources.

Psalm Types

	CORPORATE PRAISE	INDIVIDUAL PRAISE	CORPORATE LAMENT	INDIVIDUAL LAMENT
INITIAL INDICATOR	Imperative Call to Praise (e.g., "Sing to the Lord a new song")	Proclamation of Intent to Praise (e.g., "I will extol the Lord")	Vocative Opening with Petition (e.g., "Rescue us, O Lord")	Vocation Opening with Petition (e.g., "Vindicate me, O Lord")
CORE SECTION	Reason for Praise: 1. Who God Is 2. General Acts of God	Narration of Specific Intervention: 1. Describe Crisis 2. Recount Prayer 3. Report Deliverance	Lament Proper: National Crisis	Lament Proper: 1. Enemy 2. Psalmist 3. God
RESPONSE	Instruction	Acknowledge Role of God; Instruction	Petition; Confession of Trust	Petition; Optional: 1. Confession of Sin 2. Imprecation 3. Vow of Praise

Types of Hebrew Parallelism

Parallelism is the correspondence between phrases of a poetic line when the second phrase carries forward the thought of the first, but together they form a single statement.		
Semantic Parallelism (based in word usage)	Using Synonyms Using Similar Terms Using Matched Pairs Using Opposites	(2:3; 7:16; 17:1; 24:2) (1:5; 2:8; 6:1-2; 7:13; 17:8) (2:1b; 9:8; 15:1) (1:6; 15:4a; 37:9, 16)
Progressive Parallelism (based on logical sequence)	Using Cause and Effect Using Sequence Using Deduction Using Metaphors Using Explanation	(1:3; 6:7; 7:14; 16:1; 18:36; 37:4, 27) (1:1; 3:4-5; 6:10; 37:29) (4:3; 13:6; 16:8) (4:7; 18:30b) (5:10b, 11b)
Grammatical Parallelism (based on choice of grammatical forms)	Using Parallel Parts of Speech Using Word Order Using Ellipsis	(18:4-5, 25-26; 19:7-8) (reverse: 1:2; 2:5; 18:4-5) (16:11; 18:41)

Classification of Psalms
Book 1

NO.	PRAISE	LAMENT	WISDOM	INITIAL INDICATOR	TITLE	AUTHOR	OTHER CATEGORIES
1			X				
2							Royal
3		I		X	A,H	David	
4		I		X	A,M	David	
5		I		X	A,M	David	
6		I		X	A,M	David	
7		I		X	A,G,H	David	
8	C				A,M	David	
9	I/C			X	A,M	David	Acrostic (with 10)
10		I		X			Acrostic (continued)
11	I				A,M	David	
12		C		X	A,M	David	
13		I		X	A,M	David	
14			X		A,M	David	
15			X		A	David	
16		I		X	A,G	David	
17		I		X	A,G	David	
18	I			X	A,M,H	David	
19			X		A,G,M	David	
20					A,G,M	David	Royal
21					A,G,M	David	Royal
22	I:22-31	I:1-21			A,G,M	David	
23			X?		A,G	David	
24			X?		A,G	David	
25		I		X	A	David	Acrostic
26		I		X	A	David	
27	I:1-6	I:7-14			A	David	
28		I		X	A	David	
29	C			X	A,G	David	
30	I			X	A,G,H	David	
31	I		X		A,G,M	David	
32					A,G	David	Penitential
33	C			X			
34	I			X	A,H	David	Acrostic
35		I		X	A	David	Imprecatory
36			X		A,M	David	
37			X		A	David	Acrostic
38		I		X	A,G	David	
39		I			A,M	David	
40	I:1-10	I:11-17			A,G,M	David	
41		I			A,G,M	David	

Cols. 1-2: I = Individual   Col. 5: A = Author   H = Historical Context
       C = Corporate   G = Genre   M = Musical Directions

Classification of Psalms
Books 2 and 3

NO.	PRAISE	LAMENT	WISDOM	INITIAL INDICATOR	TITLE	AUTHOR	OTHER CATEGORIES
42		I		X	A,G,M	Sons of Korah	
43		I		X			
44		C		X	A,G,M	Sons of Korah	
45					A,G,M	Sons of Korah	Royal
46	C				A,G,M	Sons of Korah	
47	C			X	A,G,M	Sons of Korah	
48	C				A,G	Sons of Korah	Zion song
49			X		A,G,M	Sons of Korah	
50					A,G	Asaph	Indictment oracle
51		I		X	A,G,H,M	David	Penitential
52			X		A,G,H,M	David	
53			X		A,G,M	David	
54		I		X	A,G,H,M	David	
55		I		X	A,G,M,	David	
56		I		X	A,G,H,M	David	
57		I		X	A,G,H,M	David	
58		I			A,G,M	David	
59		I		X	A,G,H,M	David	
60		C		X	A,G,H,M	David	
61		I		X	A,M	David	
62			X		A,G,M	David	Confidence
63					A,G,H	David	Confidence
64		I		X	A,G,M	David	
65	C				A,G,M	David	
66	C			X	G,M		
67	C				G,M		
68	C				A,G,M	David	
69		I		X	A,M	David	
70		I		X	A,G,M	David	
71		I		X			
72					A	Solomon	Royal
73			X		A,G	Asaph	
74		C		X	A,G	Asaph	
75	C				A,G,M	Asaph	
76	C				A,G,M	Asaph	
77		I/C			A,G,M	Asaph	
78			X?		A,G	Asaph	Meditation on history
79		C		X	A,G	Asaph	
80		C		X	A,G,M	Asaph	
81	C			X	A,M	Asaph	National instruction
82		C?	X?		A,G	Asaph	
83		C		X	A,G	Asaph	
84	C				A,G,M	Sons of Korah	
85		C		X	A,G,M	Sons of Korah	
86		I		X	A,G	David	
87					A,G	Sons of Korah	Zion song
88		I		X	A,G,M	Sons of Korah	
89	I:1-4; C:5-18	C:38-51			A,G	Ethan	Covenant song

Cols. 1-2: I = Individual   Col. 5: A = Author   H = Historical Context
        C = Corporate   G = Genre   M = Musical Directions

Classification of Psalms
Books 4 and 5

NO.	PRAISE	LAMENT	WISDOM	INITIAL INDICATOR	TITLE	AUTHOR	OTHER CATEGORIES
90		C		X	A,G	Moses	
91							Confidence
92	I				G		
93	C						
94		I/C		X			
95	C			X			
96	C			X			
97	C						
98	C			X	G		
99	C						
100	C			X	G		
101	I			X	A,G	David	
102		I:1-11		X	G		Confidence: 12-28
103	I/C			X	A	David	
104	I/C			X			
105	C			X			Meditation on history
106	I/C:1-5			X			Meditation on history: 6-48
107	C			X			
108		C		X	A,G	David	
109		I		X	A,G,M	David	Imprecatory
110					A,G	David	Royal
111	C			X			Acrostic
112	C			X			Acrostic
113	C			X			
114							Meditation on history
115							Confidence
116	I			X			
117	C			X			
118	I/C			X			
119			X				Acrostic
120		I		X	G		Pilgrimage song
121					G		Pilgrimage; confidence
122					A,G	David	Pilgrimage song; Zion song
123					G		Pilgrimage; confidence
124	C				A,G	David	Pilgrimage song
125					G		Pilgrimage; confidence
126					G		Pilgrimage; confidence
127			X		A,G	Solomon	Pilgrimage song
128			X		G		Pilgrimage song
129		C			G		Pilgrimage; imprecatory
130		I		X	G		Pilgrimage song
131					A,G	David	Pilgrimage song
132					G		Pilgrimage; covenant
133			X		A,G	David	Pilgrimage song
134	C			X	G		Pilgrimage song
135	C			X			
136	C			X			
137		C					
138	I			X	A	David	
139		I		X	A,G,M	David	
140		I		X	A,G,M	David	
141		I		X	A,G	David	
142		I			A,G,H	David	
143		I		X	A,G	David	
144	I:1-4	I:3-15		X	A	David	Royal
145	I			X	A,G	David	Acrostic
146	I/C			X			
147	C						
148	C						
149	C						
150	C						

Cols. 1-2: I = Individual   Col. 5: A = Author   H = Historical Context
C = Corporate   G = Genre   M = Musical Directions

Psalms:
A Cantata of the Davidic Covenant

Introduction Psalms 1–2		Ps. 1. Ultimate vindication of the righteous Ps. 2. God's choice and defense of Israelite king	
BOOK	**SEAM**	**THEME**	**CONTENT**
Book 1 (1-41)	41	David's conflict with Saul	Many individual laments; most psalms mention enemies
Book 2 (42-72)	72	David's kingship	Key psalms: 45, 48, 51; 54-64 mostly laments and "enemy" psalms
Book 3 (73-89)	89	Eighth-century Assyrian crisis	Asaph and Sons of Korah collections; key psalm: 78
Book 4 (90-106)	106	Introspection about destruction of temple and exile	Praise collection: 95-100; key psalms: 90, 103-105
Book 5 (107-145)	145	Praise/reflection on return from Exile and beginning of new era	Halleluyah collection: 111-117; Songs of Ascent: 120-134; Davidic reprise: 138-145; key psalms: 107, 110, 119
Conclusion (146-150)		Climactic praise to God	

Note: This arrangement based on the conclusion that the Psalms were editorially arranged as a means of reflecting on the history of the Davidic covenant—much like songs in a cantata. For fuller discussion see Hill and Walton, *Survey of the Old Testament*.

Function of the Prophets

PERIOD	FUNCTION	AUDIENCE	MESSAGE	EXAMPLES
PRE-MONARCHY	Mouthpiece-leader	People	National guidance Maintenance of justice Spiritual overseer	Moses Deborah
				TRANSITION: Samuel
PRE-CLASSICAL	Mouthpiece-leader	King and Court	Military advice Pronouncement of rebuke or blessing	Nathan Elijah Elisha Micaiah
				TRANSITION: North—Jonah South—Isaiah
CLASSICAL	Mouthpiece-social/spiritual commentator	People	Rebuke concerning current condition of society; leads to warnings of captivity, destruction, exile, and promise of eventual restoration Call for justice and repentance	Writing prophets Best example Jeremiah

Chronology of the Prophets

	TO ISRAEL	TO JUDAH	TO FOREIGN NATION
ASSYRIAN AGE	Amos ca. 760 Hosea ca. 760-730	Isaiah ca. 740-700 Micah ca. 737-690	Jonah ca. 770
BABYLONIAN AGE		Habakkuk ca. 630 Zephaniah ca. 627 Jeremiah ca. 627-580 Daniel ca. 605-530 Ezekiel ca. 593-570	Nahum ca. 650
PERSIAN AGE		Haggai ca. 520 Zechariah ca. 520-518 Joel ca. 500 Malachi ca. 433	Obadiah ca. 500

Message and Fulfillment

MESSAGE	FULFILLMENT
Authoritative word from God ⟷	Unfolding of God's plan
Understood by prophet, relevant to contemporary audience ⟷	May be vague or obscure or take unanticipated direction
Identified with author's intention as guiding criteria ⟷	Identified often only with aid of interpreter's hindsight
Uses objective evidence ⟷	Subjective perspective
One message ⟷	Possibly many fulfillments
Does not change ⟷	May shift directions
Aim of Old Testament interpreters ⟷	Elaborated by New Testament authors

Categories of Prophetic Oracle

ORACULAR CATEGORIES	DESCRIPTION	PREEXILIC EMPHASIS	POSTEXILIC EMPHASIS
INDICTMENT	Statement of the offense	Focus primarily on idolatry, ritualism, and social justice	Focus on not giving proper honor to the Lord
JUDGMENT	Punishment to be carried out	Primarily political and projected for near future	Interprets recent or current crises as punishment
INSTRUCTION	Expected response	Very little offered; generally return to God by ending wicked conduct	Slightly more offered; more specifically addressed to particular situation
AFTERMATH	Affirmation of future hope or deliverance	Presented and understood as coming after an intervening period of judgment	Presented and understood as spanning a protracted time period Religious: now Socioeconomic: potential Political: eventual

Subjects of Aftermath Oracles

		ASSYRIAN PERIOD				BABYLONIAN PERIOD			POSTEXILIC PERIOD				TOTAL REFERENCES
TOTAL Number of Oracles = 122		Amo 2	Hos 7	Isa 28	Mica 3	Zeph 5	Jer 28	Ezk 14	Hag 2	Joel 4	Obd 1	Zech 28	
COVENANT	Regathered; Possess Land	1	2	5	1	1	18	10				2	40
	Re-elect; Holy		3	3			5	2				4	17
	Davidic King	1	1	1			3	2	1			2	11
	Multiply People			1	1		4	3					9
	Covenant Made			1	1		3	3					8
POLITICAL	Delivered by YHWH			5		1	5	2		1		4	18
	Protected by YHWH			3			2	1		1		5	12
	Defeat/Judgment Nations			4		1	4	2	1	1		5	18
	Security			5	1	1	5	3				2	17
	Peace		1	4	1		1					1	8
	Nations Coming			7	1		1					4	13
	Reunited		1				3	1					5
	YHWH Reigns			1	1	1		1				1	5
	New Leaders			1			1						2
	Pre-eminence			2	3							2	7
	Possess Enemies	1				1					1		3
	Rely on YHWH			2									2
	Law from Zion			1	1								2
	Jerusalem Rebuilt			1			4	2					7
	Jerusalem Glorified			2			1				1		4
SPIRITUAL	Sin Removed/Forgiven		1	2			3	3		1		2	12
	Ashamed of Sin			2			1	3				1	7
	YHWH in Midst			1				1		1		3	6
	Spirit Within							4		1			5
	Purge of Wicked			1		1		4				2	8
	Faithful to YHWH		1		1								2
	Fear/Serve/Worship YHWH			1			4	1				1	7
	Know YHWH			2			1	1			1		5
	Seek YHWH		1				1						2
	Reproach Removed			2		1							3
	Keep Law						1	2					3
	Temple								1			2	3
SOCIO-ECON.	Prosperity/Fertility	1	1	4			3	4		1		4	18
	Justice/Righteousness		1	3			3						7
MISC.	Cosmic Effects									2		1	3
	Nations Brought Against Jerusalem											1	1

Comparison of the Messages of the Pre-Exilic Minor Prophets

PROPHET		Object of Indictment	Nature of Indictment	Pronouncement of Judgment	Action Requested	Nature of Hope	Restoration	Kingship
ISRAEL	AMOS	All Israel (particularly upper class)	1. Injustice 2. Pagan religious practice (5:21-23)	Overrun by enemy Destruction (3:11; 5:2; 7:9; 9:8)	Justice (5:14-15, 24)	Restoration (9:11-15)	Rebuilding prosperity (9:11-15)	Messianic (9:11)
	HOSEA	All Israel	1. Pagan religious practice 2. Unfaithfulness	Covenant blessings and protection retracted	Acknowledge guilt, seek the Lord (5:15) Return (14:1)	God's faithfulness can be restored (chs. 2, 6, 14)	People will again be faithful (2:14-23)	None
JUDAH	MICAH	Leaders, prophets, and upper class (chs. 2, 3, 6)	Injustice (Secondarily idols 1:7; 5:13 or miliary strength 1:13; 5:10-11)	1. Destruction (1:16) 2. Exile	Justice (6:8)	Return of remnant 4:6-8; 5:7-8) Restoration	Dominion, peace, prosperity (ch. 4, 7)	Theocratic (4:7) Messianic (5:2)
	ZEPHANIAH	All Judah	Pagan worship (1:4-6)	Destruction	Seek the Lord (1:3)	Can avoid judgment (2:1-3) Remnant left (3:12-13)	Gathering of oppressed (3:14-20)	Theocratic (3:15)

II.

Ancient Near East

Comparative Ancient Near Eastern Chronology 10,000–2100 B.C.

ANATOLIA/SYRIA	MESOPOTAMIA		PALESTINE	EGYPT
A N C I E N T H A T T I		10000	Mesolithic: Natufian	
		8000	Neolithic Pre-pottery	
	Jarmo	5000		
	Hassuna Samarra Halaf		Neolithic Pottery Period	
		4300		Predynastic Period: Fayyum A, Deir Tasa Badarian, Amratian Gerzean
	Ubaid (4300-3500)		Chalcolithic: Ghassulian	
	South: Uruk (3500-3100) North: Tepe Gawra (3500-2900)	3300		
	Pro-literate Jemdet Nasr (3100-2900)	3000	Early Bronze I	
		2900		Protodynastic Period: Dynasties I and II (3000-2700)
	Early Dynastic I	2800	Early Bronze II	
		2700		
	Early Dynastic II	2600		
				Old Kingdom Pyramid Age Dynasties III-V (2700-2350)
	Early Dynastic III	2500	Early Bronze III	
		2400		
	Akkadian Period	2300		Dynasty VI (2350-2160)
	Gutian Period: Dynasty of Lagash	2200	Early Bronze IV	First Intermediate Period (2160-2010)
		2100		

Early Bronze IV is often assimilated into the periods surrounding it.

Comparative Ancient Near Eastern Chronology 2100-332 B.C.

ANATOLIA/SYRIA	MESOPOTAMIA		PALESTINE	EGYPT
		2100		
	Ur III Dynasty		Middle Bronze I Patriarchs	Middle Kingdom: Dynasties XI-XII (2106-1786)
		2000		
	Isin-Larsa			
		1900		
	Elam-Amorite invasions		Middle Bronze IIA sojourn	
		1800		
Old Hittite Empire (1800-1600)	Old Babylonian Period: age of Hammurabi	1700	Middle Bronze IIB & C sojourn	Second Intermediate Period: Hyksos (1786-1550)
		1600		
		1500	Late Bronze I Exodus and Conquest	New Kingdom (1550-1069): Dynasty XVIII (1550-1295)
Mitanni-Hurrian Empire (1500-1350)	Kassite Period	1400		
		1300	Late Bronze II Judges to Deborah	Dynasty XIX Empire Age (1295-1186)
Neo-Hittite Empire (1460-1200)				
		1200		
Neo-Hittites of North Syria through eighth century	Assyrian rise to power	1100	Iron I Judges and United Monarchy	Dynasty XX (1186-1069)
		1000		Dynasty XXI (1069-945)
		900		
Syrian strength till fall of Damascus 732	Assyrian Empire	800	Iron II Divided Monarchy	Late Period: Dynasties XXII-XXVI (945-525)
		700		
	Neo-Babylonian Empire	600		

PERSIAN CONTROL (539-332)

Egyptian Chronology

The Archaic Period (3000-2700)

Dynasty 1	3000-2840
Dynasty 2	2840-2700

The Old Kingdom (2700-2160)

Dynasty 3	2700-2600
Dynasty 4	2600-2500
Dynasty 5	2500-2350
Dynasty 6	2350-2190
Dynasty 7-8	2190-2160

The First Intermediate Period (2160-2010)

Dynasty 9	2160-2106
Dynasty 10	2106-2010

The Middle Kingdom (2106-1786)

Dynasty 11	2106-1963
Dynasty 12	1963-1786
Amenemhet I	*1963-1934*
Sesostris I	*1943-1898*
Amenemhet II	*1901-1866*
Sesostris II	*1868-1862*
Sesostris III	*1862-1843*
Amenemhet III	*1843-1798*
Amenemhet IV	*1798-1789*
Sobeknofru	*1789-1786*

The Second Intermediate Period (1786-1550)

Dynasty 13	1786-1633
Dynasty 14	1786-1602
Dynasties 15/16 (Hyksos)	1648-1540
Dynasty 17	1633-1550

The New Kingdom (1550-1069)

Dynasty 18	1550-1295
Ahmose I	*1550-1525*
Amenhotep I	*1525-1504*
Thutmose I	*1504-1492*
Thutmose II	*1492-1479*
Hatshepsut	*1479-1457*
Thutmose III	*1479-1425*
Amenhotep II	*1427-1400*
Thutmose IV	*1400-1390*
Amenhotep III	*1390-1352*
Amenhotep IV (Akhenaten)	*1352-1336*
Smenkhare	*1338-1336*
Tutankhamun	*1336-1327*
Ay	*1327-1323*
Haremhab	*1323-1295*
Dynasty 19	1295-1186
Rameses I	*1295-1294*
Seti I	*1294-1279*
Rameses II	*1279-1213*
Merenptah	*1213-1203*
Amenmesses	*1203-1200*
Seti II	*1200-1194*
Siptah	*1194-1188*
Tewosret	*1188-1186*

The Third Intermediate Period (1069-656)

Dynasty 20	1186-1069
Dynasty 21	1069- 945
Dynasty 22	945- 715
Sheshonq I	*945- 924*
Dynasty 23	818- 715
Dynasty 24	727- 715
Dynasty 25 (Kushite)	780- 656
Shabako	*716- 702*
Shebitku	*702- 690*
Taharqa	*690- 664*
Tantamun	*664- 656*

The Saite-Persian Period (664-332)		Dynasty 27 (Persians)	525- 404
		Dynasty 28	404- 399
Dynasty 26	664- 525	Dynasty 29	399- 380
Psammetichus I	*664- 610*	Dynasty 30	380- 343
Necho II	*610- 595*	Dynasty 31 (Persians)	343- 332
Psammetichus II	*595- 589*		
Apries (Hophra)	*589- 570*		
Amasis II	*570- 526*	**Alexander and the Ptolemies (332-30)**	
Psammetichus III	*526- 525*		

Represents the chronology of Kenneth Kitchen. See *The Anchor Bible Dictionary* II: 328–30.

Early Mesopotamian History

Early Dynastic Period (2900-2335)

Significant kings include:

Enmerkar (Uruk)	ca. 2650
Lugalbanda (Uruk)	ca. 2630
Mebaragesi (Kish)	ca. 2600
Gilgamesh (Uruk)	ca. 2600
Uruinimgina (Lagash)	ca. 2350
Lugalzagesi (Uruk)	ca. 2340

Ur III (2100-2000)

Ur-Nammu	2112-2095
Shulgi	2094-2047
Amar-Sin	2046-2038
Shu-Sin	2037-2029
Ibbi-Sin	2028-2004

Elamite Sack of Ur

The Dynasty of Akkad (2335-2200)

Sargon	2334-2279
Rimush	2278-2270
Manishtushu	2269-2255
Naram-Sin	2254-2218
Shar-kali-sharri	2217-2193

Isin-Larsa Period (2000-1750)

Ishbi-Erra (2017-1985) and his successors at Isin, including

Shu-ilishu	1984-1975
Ishme-Dagan	1953-1935
Lipit-Ishtar	1934-1924

Gungunum (1932-1906) and his successors at Larsa, including

Warad-Sin	1834-1823
Rim-Sin	1822-1763

Gutian Period

Note: Many of these dates are from J. Oates, *Babylon* (London: Thames and Hudson, 1979).

Highlights of Assyrian History

The Old Assyrian Period (2000-1750)

Shamshi-Adad I	1813-1781

controlled all of upper Mesopotamia

Eclipse of Assyria (1750-1273)

Assyria a vassal to the Hurrians
of Mitanni	1475-1400
Assur-uballit I	1365-1330

*Freedom from Mitanni and subordination
of Kassites begins development of empire*
Adad-nirari I	1307-1275

Conquered Mitanni and its vestige, Hanigalbat

The Middle Assyrian Period (1273-1076)

Tukulti-Ninurta I	1244-1208

Sack of Babylon about 1235
Tiglath-pileser I	1115-1076

Extended Assyrian control into Lebanon

Assyrian Resurgence (1076-750)

Assurnasirpal I	883- 859

*Conducted expeditions south and west, exerting
control, collecting tribute, and plundering*
Shalmaneser III	859- 823

*Established control over a number of areas
in the west, including Israel, beginning with Battle
of Qarqar in 853
Remaining kings of this period were less active
in the west and Assyrian power declined*

The Neo-Assyrian Period (750-625)

Tiglath-pileser III	745-	727
Consolidation of control over Syria	743-	738
Countered Urartian measure		
in the east	737-	735
Western campaigns to subdue Syro-Ephraimite,		
anti-Assyrian coalition	734-	732
Occupied with Chaldean rebellion	731-	729
Shalmaneser V	727-	722
Shechem captured, Tyre besieged		725
Fall of Samaria		722
Sargon II	721-	704
Battle of Der: Elam blocked Sargon's		
approach to Babylon		721
Defeat of western coalition		720
Battle with Egypt	717-	716
Campaign against Urartu		714
Subdued western revolt by Ashdod		
and Judah		712
Campaigned against Merodach-baladan		
in Babylonia	710-	707
Sennacherib	704-	681
Merodach-baladan chased from throne		
of Babylon		703
Siege of Jerusalem		701
Razing of Babylon		689
Esarhaddon	681-	669
Babylon rebuilt and control over the west		
is firm		676
Extends control over Egypt	675-	670
Assurbanipal	669-	630
Fall of Thebes		663
Aided Lydians against Cimmerians in Asia Minor		
Victory over Elamites		653
Egypt breaks free with help of Lydians		651
Rebellion in Babylon led by brother,		
Shamash-shum-ukin	650-	648
Devastation of Elam		645
Fall of Nineveh to Medes and Babylonians		612

Kings of Assyria

Ashur-uballit I	1354-1318	Shamsi-Adad V	824-810
Adad-nirari I	1318-1264	Adad-nirari III	810-782
Shalmaneser I	1264-1234	Shalmaneser IV	782-773
Tukulti-Ninurta I	1234-1197	Ashur-dan III	773-754
Ashur-dan I	1179-1133	Ashur-nirari V	754-745
Tiglath-pileser I	1115-1076	Tiglath-pileser III	745-727
Ashur-rabi II	1012-972	Shalmaneser V	727-722
Ashur-resh-ishi II	972-967	Sargon II	721-705
Tiglath-pileser II	967-935	Sennacherib	704-681
Ashur-dan II	935-912	Esarhaddon	681-669
Adad-nirari II	912-889	Ashur-banipal	669-633
Tukulti-Ninurta II	889-884	Ashur-etil-ilani	633-622
Ashur-nasir-apal II	884-858	Sin-shur-ishkun	621-612
Shalmaneser III	858-824	Ashur-uballit	612-608

Fall of Nineveh 612

Fall of Haran 610

Fall of Carchemish 605

Assyrian Foreign Policy
developed by Tiglath-pileser III

STAGE I	**Vassal relationship** Vassal committed to: — Annual payment of tribute — Furnishing of auxiliary troops
STAGE II	**If vassal was involved in Anti-Assyrian conspiracy** — Appointment of new ruler (from native royal house if representative loyal to Assyria could be found) — Territorial reductions (areas taken away were either given to loyal neighboring vassals or made into Assyrian provinces) — Deportations of parts of the upper class — Increased tribute and military presence
STAGE III	**If further Anti-Assyrian activity were even suspected** — Vassal ruler removed — Political independence revoked — Territory made into Assyrian province with Assyrian governor and officials — Deportation of upper class; replaced with foreign upper class

Kings of Israel and Judah in Assyrian Royal Inscriptions

	KING	DATE	ASSYRIAN KING	SOURCE	TRANSLATION	CONTEXT
ISRAEL	AHAB (a-ḫa-ab-bu)	853	Shalmaneser III	Kurkh Stele	ANET 279	Battle of Qarqar
	JEHU (ya-ú-a)	841	Shalmaneser III	Black Obelisk	ANET 281	Paid Tribute
	JOASH (ya-'a-su)	796	Adad-nirari III	Tell al-Rimah Stele	ANET 281f	Paid Tributre
	MENAHEM (me-ni-ḫi-im-me)	738	Tiglath-pileser III	Annals	ANET 283	Paid Tribute
	PEKAH (pa-qa-ḫa)	732	Tiglath-pileser III	Nimrud Tablet	ANET 284	Overthrown
	HOSHEA (a-ú-si-')	732	Tiglath-pileser III	Nimrud Tablet	ANET 284	Put on Throne
JUDAH	AHAZ (ya-ú-ḫa-zi)	732	Tiglath-pileser III	Nimrud Slab	ANET 282	Paid Tribute
	HEZEKIAH (ḫa-za-qi-ya-ú)	701	Sennacherib	Annals	ANET 287f	Paid Tribute
	MANASSEH (me-na-si-i)	674	Esarhaddon	Prism	ANET 291	Paid Tribute
	MANASSEH (mi-in-se-e)	unknown	Ashurbanipal	Prism C	ANET 294	Paid Tribute

Derived from A. Millard, "Israelite and Aramaean History in the Light of Inscriptions," *Tyndale Bulletin* 41-2 (1990): 271-73.
ANET = James Pritchard, *Ancient Near Eastern Texts*, 3d ed. (Princeton University Press, 1969).

Highlights of Babylonian History

The Old Babylonian Period (2000-1600)

Amorite Kings reigning in Babylon

Hammurabi	1792-1750

Famous for collection of laws

After the deaths of Shamshi-Adad of Assyria and Rim-Sin of Larsa, was able to unify and control much of Mesopotamia

Hittite sack of Babylon	1595

The Kassite Period (1600-1160)

Kassites began to rule in parts of Babylonia within a decade of Hammurabi's death

By 1460 Sealand-controlled territory in Babylonia was conquered

Period of peaceful alliances and active trade

Sack of Babylon by Tukulti-Ninurta I of Assyria	1235
Elamites bring end to Kassite rule	1160-1157

The Middle Babylonian Period (1160-730)

Nebuchadnezzar I	1126-1105

conducted successful campaign against Elam

Assyrian Domination (730-625)

Tiglath-pileser III of Assyria

Took control of Babylon in 729

Merodach-baladan	722-710, 703
Became king of Sealand	*729*
Seized control of Babylon	*722*
Ousted by Sargon, but escaped	*710*

Took throne again when Sennacherib succeeded his father; ousted a few months later	*703*
Sennacherib of Assyria completed successful siege of Babylon and razed the city	*689*
Babylon rebuilt by Sennacherib's son, Esarhaddon	*676*

The Neo-Babylonian Period (625-539)

Nabopolassar	626-605
Established Babylonian independence from Assyria	
Entered alliance with Medes after the fall of Assur	*614*
Alliance brought fall of Nineveh	*612*
Fall of Haran	*610*
Dissolution of the Assyrian state with the fall of Carchemish	*605*
Nebuchadnezzar	605-562
Extended Babylonian control into the west with defeat of Ashkelon	*604*
Unsuccessful attempt to raid Egypt	*601*
After brief revolt, Jerusalem surrendered, Jehoiachin deported	*597*
Fall of Jerusalem, destruction of Temple	*587*
Nabonidus	555-539
Undertook religious reform in devotion to the moon god, Sin	
Installed son, Belshazzar, as regent and spent 10 years in Teima	*550*
Babylon opens gates to Persian king, Cyrus	*539*

Kings of Syria

KING	DATES	SCRIPTURE
Hezion (Rezon)	940-915	1 Kings 11:23-25; 15:18
Tabrimmon	915-900	1 Kings 15:18
Benhadad I	900-860	1 Kings 15:18, 20
Benhadad II	860-841	1 Kings 20
Hazael	841-806	2 Kings 8:15
Benhadad III	806-770	2 Kings 13:3
Rezin	750-732	2 Kings 15:37

Kings of Neo-Babylonia

KING	DATES	SCRIPTURE
Nabopolassar	625-605	
Nebuchadnezzar	605-562	2 Kings 24-25; Daniel
Amel-Marduk (Evil-Merodach)	562-560	2 Kings 25:27-30; Jer. 52:31-34
Neriglissar	560-556	Jer. 39:3, 13
Labashi-Marduk	556	
Nabonidus (Nabunaid)	556-539	

Chronology of the Persian Period

PERSIAN KING	DATES	BIBLICAL CORRELATION	GREEK CORRELATION
CYRUS	539-530	Return of Zerubbabel and Jeshua (Ezra 1-3)	
CAMBYSES	530-522	Rebuilding at Jerusalem stopped (Ezra 4)	
DARIUS I	522-486	Haggai and Zechariah prophesy (520) Temple completed (516) (Ezra 5-6)	Greeks defeat Persians at Marathon (490)
XERXES	486-464	Story of Esther (Esther 1-9)	Greeks defeat Persians at Thermopolae (480 and Salamis (479) Herodotus 485-425
ARTAXERXES I	464-423	Return of Ezra (458) (Ezra 7-10) Return of Nehemiah (445) (Nehemiah 1-2) Prophecy of Malachi (433)	Golden Age (461-431) Pericles (460-429) Athens rules
DARIUS II	423-404	B I B L I C A L S I L E N C E	Peloponnesian Wars (431-404) Athens falls (404) Sparta rules
ARTAXERXES II	404-359		Socrates (470-399) Plato (428-348) Aristotle (384-322)
ARTAXERXES III	359-338		Philip II of Macedon defeats Greeks at Chaeronea in 338
ARSES	338-335		
DARIUS III	335-331		Alexander the Great overthrows Persian Empire
ALEXANDER	336-323		Establishment of Greek Empire

Israel's Neighbors
(From the Exodus until the Division of the Empire)

Period	EDOM	MOAB	AMMON	AMALEK
FATHER	Esau: son of Isaac	Moab: son of Lot and his eldest daughter	Ben-Ammi: son of Lot and his second daughter	Amalek: son of Eliphaz, who was a son of Esau
EXODUS	The country was controlled to some degree by Amorites. Refused passage to the Israelites (Num. 20:14-21)	The country was conquered by Sihon and the Amorites (Num. 21:26) King Balak feared Israel and sought the services of Balaa to curse them (Num. 22)		Defeated by the Israelites at Rephidim (Exod. 17:8-16) Defeated the Israelites at Hormah following report of the spies (Num. 14:45)
JUDGES	c. 1350 Continued under the partial control of the Amorites (Judg. 1:35-36)	c. 1350 King Eglon oppressed Israel for 18 years Ehud delivered Israel by assassinating Eglon (Judg. 3:12-30)	c. 1350 Ally of Eglon of Moab c. 1100 B.C. Oppressed Israel for 18 years. Defeated by Jephthah (Judg. 10-12)	c. 1350 Ally of Eglon of Moab
UNITED MONARCHY	c. 1030 Saul took some cities from Edomite territory (1 Sam. 14:47) c. 1000 Conquered and subjugated by David (1 Chron. 18:12)	c. 1030 Saul took some cities from Moabite territory (1 Sam. 14:47) c. 1000 Conquered and subjugated by David (2 Sam. 8:2)	c. 1050 Nahash defeated by Saul at Jabesh-gilead (1 Sam. 11:1-11) c. 1030 Saul took some cities from Ammonite territory (1 Sam. 14:47) c. 990 Hanun defeated by David; Rabbah captured; Ammon subjugated (2 Sam. 12:26-31)	c. 1020 Agag defeated by Saul in southwest Palestine. Saul failed to destroy Amalek totally as the Lord had commanded (1 Sam. 15:1-9) c. 1010 Destroyed David's camp at Ziklag while he was gone. David pursued and wiped them out. This is last mention of them (1 Sam. 30)

Israel's Neighbors
(From Division of Kingdom until Babylonian Conquest)

MOAB	AMMON	EDOM
930—At the time of division, all were subjugated to the nation of Israel		
925—Revolted during reign of Jeroboam and gained freedom	925—Declared freedom from Jeroboam	Remained under the control of Judah
877—Subjugated by Omri	853—Baasha of Ammon allied with Ahab and others against Assyria at Qarqar	
Coalition against Jehoshaphat in 853 defeated at En-gedi (2 Chron. 20:1)		
850—King Mesha revolted against Jehoram of Israel and gained freedom (2 Kings 3:4-27)	Retained freedom	845—Revolted against Jehoram of Judah and gained freedom (2 Chron. 21:8-10)
		794—Defeated by Amaziah (2 Chron. 25:11-13)
780—Uzziah and Jeroboam II subjugated all three		
Remained subjugated	738—Gained freedom from Jotham (2 Chron. 27:5)	735—Gained freedom from Ahaz (2 Chron. 28:17)
732—All became Assyrian tributaries		
711—Conquered by Sargon	Remained as Assyrian tributaries	
690—Rebellion suppressed by Sennacherib		
612—Gained partial freedom with fall of Nineveh—607—Raided Judah for Babylon		
605—Subjugated by Nebuchadnezzar 581—Rebelled and was conquered	581—King Baalis rebelled and was conquered	601—Became and remained Babylonian tributary

Israel's Neighbors

	PHOENICIA	PHILISTIA
ORIGIN	Semitic Amorites	Aegean Sea people
PRE-JUDGES	c. 1500 Territory was divided between Hittite and Egyptian domination	Not yet in Palestine
JUDGES	1400—Began slow rebellion, first against Egypt 1380-1287—Mostly controlled by Hittites; control diminished until 1190 1190—Invasion by sea peoples. Independent city-states established 1100—Some control exercised by Tiglath-pileser I	1190—Defeated Hittites, destroyed capital. Defeated by Rameses III, settled on coast of Palestine. Five major cities: Gath, Gaza, Ashkelon, Ashdod, Ekron 11th cent—Controlled parts of at least Dan and Judah (Judg. 14:4; 15:11). Samson held somewhat in control 1060—Overran Israel; captured ark (1 Sam. 4) 1050—Israel subdued Philistia at Ebenezer (1 Sam. 7:7-14)
SAUL	Political independence; cultural development	Philistines held in check through most of this period. They were defeated at Michmash by Jonathan and at Elah through David. Overran country at end after defeating and killing Saul at Mt. Gilboa
1000–900 B.C.	Golden Age 981-942—Hiram I of Tyre; alliance with Israel. Expansion of sea trade and exploration; colonie in N. Africa, Spain, Asia Minor, and Mediterranean	David defeated and subdued the Philistines (2 Sam. 5:17-25)
900–722 B.C.	890—High Priest Ethbaal gains throne. Alliance with Israel continues with marriage of his daughter Jezebel to Ahab 865—Paid tribute to Assyria—Ashur-nasir-pal II 853—Joined 12-nation alliance against Shalmaneser III at Qarqar 841—Shalmaneser III takes some cities. Assyrian tributary through end of period	Paid tribute to Jehoshaphat (2 Chron. 17:11) Raided Judah during the reign of Jehoram (2 Chron. 21:16-17) 805—Assyrian Adad-nirari III collected tribute; subjugated by Uzziah but invaded Judah during reign of Ahaz (2 Chron. 28:18); subdued by Tiglath-pileser III of Assyria
722–570 B.C.	725—During reign of Shalmaneser V, Luli of Sidon tried to unite Phoenicia in revolt 701—Sennacherib responded by invasion—many cities taken, deportation, puppet ruler 677—Revolt crushed by Esarhaddon—Sidon destroyed 665—Baalit of Tyre revolted—suppressed by Ashurbanipal 584-571—Nebuchadnezzar besieged & took Tyre	Country subjugated and Gaza captured by Hezekiah (2 Kings 18:8) People captured and deported by Nebuchadnezzar

The Nations in Prophecy
(prophets listed in chronological order)

	AMOS	ISAIAH	JEREMIAH	EZEKIEL	MISCELLANEOUS
BABYLON		13:1-14:23 Destruction: like Sodom and Gomorrah; no survivors	50-51 Captivity; destruction; humiliation; desolation; ruin		Habakkuk 2:6-17: Destruction; disgrace
PHILISTIA	1:6-8 Remnant will perish; destruction	14:29-32 Helpless famine; defeated from north	47 Conquered from north; destruction; mourning remnant	25:15-17 Destruction; remnant cut off	
MOAB	2:1-3 Fire; death	15-16 Devastation; ruin; mourning; some remnant	48 Desolation; shame; exile; laughingstock; future restoration	25:8-11 Captivity	
DAMASCUS	1:3-5 Cut off; exile	17:1-3 Ruin, but a remnant left	49:23-27 Helpless; destruction		
EGYPT		19 Civil war; economic decline; military defeat; conquered by Assyria	46:1-26 To be conquered by Nebuchadnezzar	29-32 Overcome by Babylon	
EDOM	1:11-12 Fire	21:11-12 Devastation; but possibility of survival	49:7-22 Flight; ruin; object of horror; like Sodom and Gomorrah; desolation	25:12-14 Laid waste	Obadiah: Destruction; no survivors
TYRE	1:9-10 Burning of citadels	23 Destruction; conquest; restoration after 70 years.		26-28 Overthrown; mourning; destruction	
AMMON	1:13-15 Exile		49:1-6 Desolate heap possessed by Israel; exile; future restoration	25:1-7 Destruction	
NINEVEH					Nahum: Control of Judah ended; besieged, destroyed, plundered

Intertestamental Chronology
(dates B.C.)

SELEUCIDS	PTOLEMIES	MACCABEANS
Seleucus I 312-281	Ptolemy I Soter 323-285	Mattathias 168-166
Antiochus I 281-261	Ptolemy II Philadelphus 285-247	Judas Maccabeus 166-160
Antiochus II 261-246	Ptolemy III Euergetes 247-222	Jonathan Maccabeus 160-143
Seleucus II 246-226	Ptolemy IV Philapator 222-205	Simon Maccabeus 143-135
Seleucus III 226-223	Ptolemy V Epiphanes 205-182	John Hyrcanus I 135-104
Antiochus III 223-187	Ptolemy VI Philometer 182-146	Aristobulus I 104-103
Seleucus IV Philapator 187-175	Ptolemy VII Euergetes II 146-116	Alexander Jannaeus 103-76
Antiochus IV Epiphanes 175-163	Ptolemy VIII Soter II 116-108	Hyrcanus II and Alexandra 76-67
Antiochus V Eupator 163-162	Ptolemy IX Alexander 108-89	Hyrcanus II and
Demetrius I Soter 162-150	Ptolemy VIII Soter II 88-80	Aristobulus II 67-63
Alexander Balas 150-145	Ptolemy X Alexander II 80	Pompey called in 63
Demetrius II Nicator 145-139	End of Legitimate Ptolemaic Line	Antipater 55-43
Antiochus VII 139-129		Herod the Great 40-4

Major Inscriptions of Old Testament Significance

NAME	LANGUAGE	DISCOVERER	LOCATION FOUND	DATE FOUND	SUBJECT	DATE OF ORIGIN	BIBLICAL SIGNIFICANCE
Beni Hasan Tomb Painting	Hieroglyphic	Newberry	Beni Hasan	1902	Tomb painting of Khnumhotep II	1900	Pictures Semites in Egypt
Laws of Hammurabi	Akkadian (Old Babylonian)	deMorgan	Susa	1901	Collection of Babylonian laws	1725	Illustrates ancient Near Eastern law
Merenptah Stela	Hieroglyphic	Petrie	Thebes	1896	Military accomplishments of Merenptah	1207	First mention of the name "Israel"
Sheshonq Inscription	Hieroglyphic		Karnak Temple	1825	Military accomplishments of Sheshonq	920	Confirmation of raid against Rehoboam
"House of David" Inscription*	Aramaic	Biran	Dan	1993	Syrian conquest of region	9th c.	Earliest mention of David in contemporary records
Mesha Inscription	Moabite	Klein	Dibon	1868	Military accomplishments of Mesha of Moab	850	Moabite-Israelite relations in 9th century
Black Stela	Akkadian (Neo-Assyrian)	Layard	Nineveh	1845	Military accomplishments of Shalmaneser III	840	Picture Israelites paying tribute
Balaam Texts	Aramaic	Franken	Deir Alla (Succoth)	1967	Prophecy of Balaam about the displeasure of the divine council	8th c.	Connected to a famous seer known from the Bible
Silver Scrolls	Hebrew	Barkay	Hinnom Valley Tomb	1979	Amulet containing the text of Num: 6:24-26	7th c.	Earliest copy of any portion of the Bible
Siloam Inscription	Hebrew	Peasant boy	Jerusalem	1880	Commemoration of the completion of Hezekiah's water tunnel	701	Contemporary example of Hebrew language
Sennacherib Cylinder	Akkadian (Neo-Assyrian)	Taylor	Nineveh	1830	Military accomplishments of Sennacherib	686	Describes siege of Jerusalem
Lachish Ostraca	Hebrew	Starkey	Tell ed-Duweir	1935	18 letters from the captain of the fort of Lachish	588	Conditions during the final Babylonian siege
Cyrus Cylinder	Akkadian	Rassam	Babylon	1879	Decree of Cyrus allowing the rebuilding of temples	535	Illustrates the policy by which Judah also benefitted

*Reading disputed; see *Biblical Archaeology Review*, July/Aug. 1994.

Major Tablets
of Old Testament Significance

NAME	NUMBER OF TABLETS	LANGUAGE	DISCOVERER	LOCATION FOUND	DATE FOUND	SUBJECT	DATE OF ORIGIN	BIBLICAL SIGNIFICANCE
Ebla	17,000	Eblaite	Matthiae	Tell-Mardikh	1976	Royal archives containing many types of texts	24th c.	Provide historical background of Syria in late 3rd millennium
Atrahasis	3	Akkadian	Many found different parts	different parts in different sites	1889 to 1967	Account of creation, population growth, and flood	1635 copy	Parallels to Genesis accounts
Mari	20,000	Akkadian (Old Babylonian)	Parrot	Tell-Hariri	1933	Royal archives of Zimri-Lim containing many types of texts	18th c.	Provide historical background of the period and largest collection of prophetic texts
Enuma Elish	7	Akkadian (Neo-Assyrian)	Layard	Nineveh (library of Ashurbanipal)	1848-1876	Account of Marduk's ascension to the head of the pantheon	7th c. copy	Parallels to Genesis creation accounts
Gilgamesh	12	Akkadian (Neo-Assyrian)	Rassam	Nineveh (library of Ashurbanipal)	1853	The exploits of Gilgamesh and Enkidu and the search for immortality	7th c. copy	Parallels to Genesis flood accounts
Boghaz-Köy	10,000	Hittite	Winckler	Boghaz-Köy	1906	Royal archives of the Neo-Hittite Empire	16th c.	Hittite history and illustrations of international treaties
Nuzi	4000	Hurrian dialect of Akkadian	Chiera and Speiser	Yorghun Tepe	1925 to 1941	Archive containing family records	15th c.	Source for contemporary customs in mid-2nd millennium
Ugarit	1400	Ugaritic	Schaeffer	Ras Shamra	1929 to 1937	Royal archives of Ugarit	15th c.	Canaanite religion and literature
Amarna	380	Akkadian (W. Semitic dialect)	Egyptian peasant	Tell el-Amarna	1887	Correspondence between Egypt and her vassals in Canaan	1360 to 1330	Reflects conditions in Palestine in the mid-2nd millennium
Babylonian Chronicles	4	Akkadian (Neo-Babylonian)	Wiseman	Babylon	1956	Court records of Neo-Babylonian Empire	626 to 594	Record of capture of Jerusalem in 597 and history of the period

Archaeological Periods

ARCHAEOLOGICAL PERIODS IN PALESTINE	APPROXI-MATE DATES B.C.	EGYPTIAN DYNASTIES	APPROXI-MATE DATES B.C.	BIBLICAL CORRELATIONS	APPROXIMATE DATES B.C. (early chronology)
Neolithic Pre-pottery Neolithic Pottery	8000-6000 6000-4300				
Chalcolithic	4300-3300	Badarian, Nagada	3900-3300		
Early Bronze I Early Bronze II Early Bronze III Early Bronze IV	3300-2900 2900-2600 2600-2300 2300-2100	I and II III to V (Pyramid Age) First Intermediate Period (VII-X)	3000-2700 2700-2350 2190-2010	Post Flood	
Middle Bronze I Middle Bronze IIA Middle Bronze IIB Middle Bronze IIC	2100-1900 1900-1700 1700-1600 1600-1550	XII Second Intermediate Period Hyksos	1963-1786 1786-1550 1648-1540	Patriarchs Sojourn in Egypt	2150-1850 1876-1446
Late Bronze I Late Bronze IIA Late Bronze IIB	1550-1400 1400-1300 1300-1200	New Kingdom XVIII Empire Age XIX	1550-1295 1295-1186	Conquest Judges	1406-1400 1400-1050
Iron IA Iron IB Iron IC	1200-1150 1150-1000 1000-918	XXI	1069-945	United Monarchy	1050-930
Iron IIA Iron IIB	918-800 800-586	XXII XXVI	945-715 664-525	Divided Monarchy	930-586
Iron III	586-332			Captivity	586-539

Development of Warfare

<table>
<tr><th colspan="2">ITEMS</th><th>MIDDLE BRONZE</th><th>LATE BRONZE</th><th>IRON I</th><th>IRON II</th></tr>
<tr><td rowspan="2">CHRONOLOGICAL DATA</td><td>DATES INVOLVED</td><td>2100-1550</td><td>1550-1200</td><td>1200-918</td><td>918-586</td></tr>
<tr><td>BIBLICAL PERIOD</td><td>Patriarchs and Egyptian sojourn</td><td>Egyptian sojourn, conquest, and judges</td><td>Judges and united monarchy</td><td>Divided monarchy</td></tr>
<tr><td rowspan="4">WEAPONS</td><td>AXE</td><td>Eye axe, duckbill axe (mostly socket)</td><td>Pronged socket axe</td><td>Rectangular socket axe</td><td>Nearly obsolete</td></tr>
<tr><td>SWORD</td><td>Short sickle sword; spined, two-edged sword</td><td>Long sickle sword</td><td>Longer, straight two-edged; some long sickle</td><td>Mostly straight, long, and spined</td></tr>
<tr><td>BOW</td><td>Simple bow: double convex and single arc</td><td>Mostly composite bow: triangular and recurved</td><td>Composite bow</td><td>Improved composite bow: ends curve back</td></tr>
<tr><td>SPEAR</td><td>Tang type</td><td>Socket</td><td>Socket</td><td>Socket</td></tr>
<tr><td>CITY DEFENSE</td><td>GATE</td><td>"L" type or three-pilaster</td><td>Two-chamber with towers</td><td>Three-chamber with towers</td><td>One-chamber with towers</td></tr>
<tr><td>MOBILITY</td><td>CHARIOT</td><td>Light, stone and wood, and spoked wheels</td><td>Lighter, all wood, and four spokes</td><td>Heavier and more solid, six spokes, and axle at back</td><td>Bigger, more horses (three or four) eight spokes, and axle at back</td></tr>
</table>

Comparison of Biblical and Babylonian Creation Accounts

GENESIS ACCOUNT	ENUMA ELISH
God is seen as ultimate source of power; transcends creation.	Magic incantations are ultimate source of power; the gods are subject to nature. III. 101; IV. 1-26, 91*
Organized coverage of creation; systematically includes general realms of nature.	Does not include creation of vegetation, animals or light—the existence of these is assumed. Moon and stars created, but not sun. V. 2-22
Purpose: Praise to God as Lord of creation; acknowledging Him as such. A tribute to God's ultimacy and authority.	Purpose: Hymn of praise to Marduk as champion and mightiest of the gods. Creation is incidental. VI. 100ff.
Begins before things as we know them existed (Gen. 1:1); as God created, He gave names. Gen. 1:5, 8, 10	Begins before heaven and earth were *named*; cannot imagine situation before they existed. I. 1-2
Starts with primeval deep. Hebrew: *tehom* Gen. 1:2	Starts with the deep—fresh water (Apsu) and salt water (Tiamat—cognate of *tehom*). I. 3-4
Creation given time sequence; set in blocks by "days." Gen. 1:5, 8, 13, etc.	No chronological structure of "days."
Creation by speech. Gen. 1:3, 6, 9, 11, 20	Creation from formerly existing matter. IV. 137-140; VI. 33
Waters separated above and below by firmament. Gen. 1:6-8	Corpse of Tiamat divided in two and set up as waters above and below. IV. 137-140
Man created to rule creation. Gen. 1:28	Man created to do the service of the gods so the gods wouldn't have to work so hard. VI, 8, 34
Man created from the soil. Gen. 2:7	Man created from blood of slain hero (Kingu). VI. 33

*Enuma Elish references designate tablet number and line.

Comparison of Biblical and Babylonian Flood Accounts

ITEM	GENESIS ACCOUNT	GILGAMESH EPIC
Flood divinely planned	Planned by God	Planned at council of gods Anu, Enlil, Ninurta, Ennugi, Ea, Ishtar
Divine revelation of plan to hero	God wanted to spare Noah because of his righteousness	Ea warned hero, Utnapishtim, in a dream
Reason for flood	Sin of man	Noise of man disturbed the gods' rest
Punishment	Highly ethical and just	Ethically ambiguous and later regretted
Salvation of hero	Included in God's plan	Done secretly
Life saved	8 persons (family), representatives of each animal	Representatives of all living things, beasts, several families, craftsmen, and technicians
Building of boat	Flat-bottomed, rectangular, 300 x 50 x 30 cubits, 3 levels, door, window, pitch coating	Ziggurat-shaped, 120 x 120 x 120 cubits, 7 levels, 9 sections, door, window, pitch coating
Physical causes of flood	More comprehensive: land upheavals, subterranean waters, heavy rains	Rains, winds, breaking of dikes
Duration of flood	40 days, 40 nights	6 days and nights
Landing of boat	Mountains of Ararat	Mount Nisir
Sending of birds	Raven, dove (3 times)	Dove, swallow, raven
Acts of worship	Sacrifice of worship	Sacrifice for appeasement
Blessing of hero	Earthly covenant	Divinity, immortality

Ancient Near Eastern Literature Containing Parallels to the Old Testament

LITERARY WORK	LANGUAGE	DATE	OT BOOK	NATURE OF PARALLEL
Atrahasis Epic	Akkadian	~1635	Genesis	Creation, population growth, and flood with ark
Enuma Elish[1]	Akkadian	~1100	Genesis	Account of Creation
Gilgamesh Epic[2]	Sumerian Akkadian	~2000	Genesis	Account of the Flood complete with ark and birds
Memphite Theology	Egyptian	~13th c.	Genesis	Creation by spoken word
Hammurabi's Laws	Akkadian	~1750	Exodus	Laws similar to those given at Sinai in form and content
Hymn to the Aten	Egyptian	~1375	Psalm 104	Wording used in motifs and analogies; subject matter
Ludlul bel Nemeqi	Akkadian	~13th c.	Job	Sufferer questions justice of deity
Babylonian Theodicy	Akkadian	~1000	Job	Dialogue between sufferer and friend concerning the justice of deity
Instruction of Amenemope	Egyptian	~1200	Proverbs 22:17-24:22	Vocabulary, imagery, subject matter, structure
Hittite Treaties (36)[3]	Hittite	2nd m.	Deuteronomy Joshua 24	Format and content
Lamentations over the fall of Sumerian Cities (5)	Sumerian	20th c.	Lamentations	Phrasing, imagery, and subject matter
Egyptian Love Songs (54)	Egyptian	1300-1150	Song of Solomon	Content and literary categories employed
Mari Prophecy Texts (~50)	Akkadian	18th c.	Preclassical Prophecy[4]	Addressed similar subjects (military undertakings and cultic activity)

1 See chart on p. 80 Comparison of Biblical and Babylonian Creation Accounts
2 See chart on p. 81: Comparison of Biblical and Babylonian Flood Accounts
3 See chart on p. 86: Treaty Format and Biblical Covenants

Ancient Near Eastern Deities

DEITY	COUNTRY	POSITION	REFERENCE	
Baal	Canaan	Young storm god	I Kings 16:31; 18:18-46	
Ashtoreth (Astarte)	Canaan	Mother-goddess; love; fertility	Judg. 2:13; 10:6; I Sam. 12:10; I Kings 11:5	
Chemosh	Moab	National god of war	Num. 21:29; Judg. 11:24; I Kings 11:7, 33; Jer. 48:7	
Molech (Malcam, Milcom)	Ammon	National god	Zeph. 1:5; Jer. 49:1; I Kings 11:5, 7, 33	
Dagon	Philistia	National god of grain	Judg. 16:23; I Sam. 5:2-7	
Queen of Heaven	Canaan	Same as Ashtoreth (similar to Anat and Ishtar)	Jer. 7:18; 44:17-25	Palestinian Deities in Scripture

DEITY	COUNTRY	POSITION	REFERENCE	
Marduk	Babylon	Young storm god; chief god	Jer. 50:2	
Bel	Babylon	Another name for Marduk	Isa. 46:1; Jer. 50:2; 51:44	
Nebo (Nabu)	Babylon	Son of Marduk	Isa. 46:1	
Tammuz (Dumuzi)	Sumerian	Young storm god	Ezek. 8:14	Mesopotamian Deities in Scripture

EGYPT	MESOPOTAMIA	CANAAN-SYRIA	
Osiris—death Isis—life Horus—sun Hathor—mother goddess Re—sun Seth—evil; storm Ptah—artists; Memphite creator	Anu—head of pantheon Enlil—storm Ea-Enki—fresh water and subterranean water Sin (Nanna)—moon Ishtar—sex, fertility Ninurta—war Tiamat—salt water	El—head of Canaanite pantheon Anat—war Mot—death, sterility Adad—Syrian storm god Teshub—Hittite storm god Hannahanna—Hittite mother goddess Arinna—Hittite sun goddess	Major Deities not in Scripture

Deities of these civilizations, particularly Egypt, vary as to attributes and rank, depending on the time period and the areas of the country. The ones listed are basic.

Key Theological Distinctions
Between Israel and Her Neighbors

ISSUE	ISRAEL IDEAL	PAGAN POLYTHEISM
Ultimacy of deity	Yahweh is the ultimate power in the universe. He answers to no one and there are no limitations on his jurisdiction.	The gods have competing agendas and limited jurisdiction. Even as a corporate body they do not exercise ultimate sovereignty.
Manifestation of deity	Yahweh cannot be represented in material form or in the form of any natural phenomena.	Deities represented iconically, anthropomorphically, or in natural phenomena.
Disposition of deity	Yahweh is consistent in character and has bound himself by his attributes.	Deity is not bound by any code of conduct. Inconsistent, unpredictable and accountable only marginally to the divine assembly.
Autonomy of deity	Yahweh is not dependent on people for the provision of any needs.	People provided food and housing for deity (sacrifices and temples).
Requirements of deity	Made known in detail through the giving of the law.	Not revealed; could only be inferred from one's fortunes.
Response to deity	Yahweh expects conformity to the Law and to his holiness and justice.	Ritualistic, though maintaining an ordered society was important.
Creation of the cosmos	Yahweh undertook and sovereignly executed a cohesive plan of creation.	Accomplished by procreation of the gods, with no directing influence and was organized and established through conflict between the gods.
Human dignity	Derived from being created in the image of God and placed over creation. Yahweh created for people and with people in mind.	Since humans were a bother and an afterthought, created as slaves, dignity derived from the belief that they provided the needs of the gods.
Revelation	Yahweh's will, purposes, and nature were a matter of public record provided by Yahweh.	The will, purposes, and nature of deity could only be inferred.
Election	Israel understood herself to be the elect people of God.	Occasionally a king or dynasty was considered elect, but no sustained doctrine of election existed.
Historiography	History recorded as a means of Yahweh's revelation and therefore didactic.	History recorded as a means of propagandistic justification and certification of the current regime.
Divine intervention	Directed toward an established and consistent goal in keeping with Yahweh's intention of revealing himself and his attributes.	Directed toward maintaining a *status quo* or returning to a previous *status quo* and is primarily *ad hoc*.
Omens	Worldview of Israel rejected omen mentality.	Viewed as indicating whether the gods were bringing favorable or unfavorable circumstances.
Incantations	Worldview of Israel rejected manipulation of deity by incantations.	Incantations used as a magical means of coercing deity to respond in desired ways.

The Plagues
and the Gods of Egypt

PLAGUE	REFERENCE	POSSIBLE EGYPTIAN DEITY DIRECTED AGAINST
NILE TURNED TO BLOOD	Exodus 7:14-25	Khnum: guardian of the Nile Hapi: spirit of the Nile Osiris: Nile was bloodstream
FROGS	Exodus 8:1-15	Heqt: form of frog; god of resurrection
GNATS (MOSQUITOES)	Exodus 8:16-19	
FLIES	Exodus 8:20-32	
PLAGUE ON CATTLE	Exodus 9:1-7	Hathor: mother-goddess; form of cow Apis: bull of god Ptah; symbol of fertility Mnevis: sacred bull of Heliopolis
BOILS	Exodus 9:8-12	*Imhotep: god of medicine
HAIL	Exodus 9:13-35	Nut: sky goddess Isis: goddess of life Seth: protector of crops
LOCUSTS	Exodus 10:1-20	Isis: goddess of life Seth: protector of crops
DARKNESS	Exodus 10:21-29	Re, Aten, Atum, Horus: all sun gods of sorts
DEATH OF FIRSTBORN	Exodus 11:1-12:36	The deity of Pharaoh: Osiris, the giver of life

These are only some of the gods whom the plagues may have been directed against. It is not necessarily conclusive.
*Perhaps too early for this deity to have been involved.

Treaty Format and Biblical Covenants

ORDER OF SECTIONS IN HITTITE TREATIES (2nd millennium)	DESCRIPTION	EXOD.-LEV.	DEUT.	JOSH. 24
INTRODUCTION OF SPEAKER	Identifying author and his right to proclaim treaty	Exod. 20:1	1:1-5	Vv. 1-2
HISTORICAL PROLOGUE	Survey of past relationship between parties	20:2	1:6-3:29	Vv. 2-13
STIPULATIONS	Listing of obligations	Decalogue 20:1-17 Covenant code 20:22-23:19 Ritual 34:10-26 Lev. 1-25	Chs. 4-26	Vv. 14-25
STATEMENT CONCERNING DOCUMENT	Storage and public reading instructions	Exod. 25:16?	27:2-3	V. 26
WITNESSES	Usually identifying the gods who are called to witness the oath	None	Chs. 31-32	Vv. 22, 27
CURSES AND BLESSINGS	How deity will respond to adherence to or violation of treaty	Lev. 26:1-33	Ch. 28	V. 20

Legal Texts
of the Ancient Near East

	NAME	CENTURY B.C.	DESCRIPTION
SUMERIAN	Reform of Uruinimgina (King of Lagash)	24th (E.D.III)	Social reform
	Laws of Ur-Nammu (King of Ur)	21st	About 31 laws remain. Fragmented
	Laws of Lipit-Ishtar (King of Isin)	19th (Isin-Larsa)	Parts of 38 laws with prologue and epilogue: civil law only
AKKADIAN	Laws of Eshnunna	18th (Old Babylonian)	60 paragraphs civil and criminal law
	Laws of Hammurabi (King of Babylon)	18th (Old Babylonian)	282 Laws remaining (35-40 erased) plus prologue and epilogue
	Middle Assyrian laws (Tiglath-Pileser I?)	12th (Middle Assyrian)	About 100 laws on 11 tablets civil and criminal law
HITTITE	Hittite laws (Murshilish I or Khattushilish I)	17th (Old Hittite)	About 200 laws civil and criminal law

III.

Bible Study

The Semitic Language Family

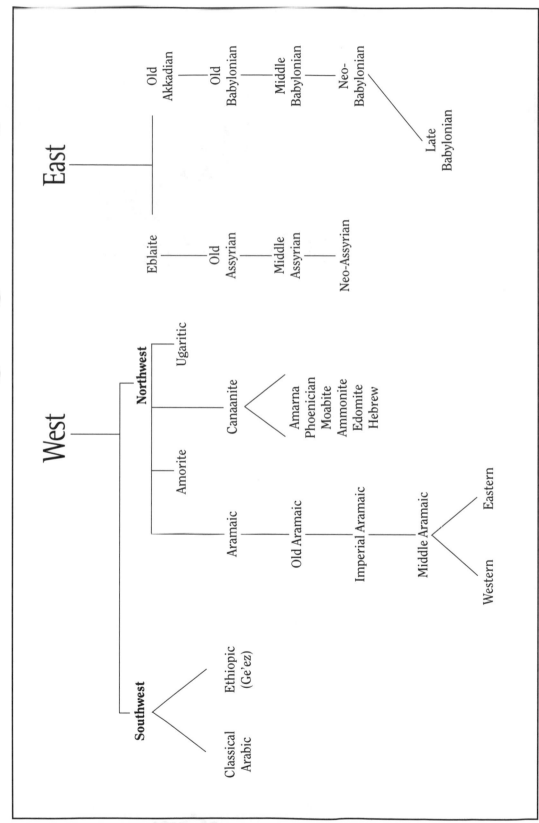

Versions and Manuscripts of the Old Testament

VERSIONS BASED ON HEBREW	MSS OF HEBREW TEXT		VERSIONS BASED ON GREEK LXX	REVISIONS OF GREEK	MSS OF GREEK TEXT
Septuagint (Greek)	Dead Sea Scrolls	200			Rylands 458 Fouad 266 "Kaige"
Samaritan Pentateuch		100			Dead Sea Scrolls
	Nash Papy.				
		AD BC			
		100		Aquila	Chester
			Old Latin	Symmachus Theodotion	Beatty Papy. 967-968
Peshitta (Syriac)		200			Papy. 911
Targum Onkelos (Aramaic)			Coptic	Origen's Hexapla	Washington Vaticanus
Targum Jonathan Vulgate (Latin)		300			Sinaiticus
			Ethiopic	Lucian	
		400			
		500			Alexandrinus
Targum Pseudo-Jonathan		600			Marchalianus
			Syro-Hexaplar		
		700			
	BM 4445 Cairo	800			Bodleianus
	Leningrad Aleppo	900			
	Leningrad	1000			

Textual Criticism: Types of Errors

TYPE OF ERROR	DESCRIPTION	EXAMPLE
Letter confusion	Two letters look alike	Jer. 15:14 צבר/צֶבַד ('br/'bd)
Hearing confusion	Two words or letters sound alike	לוֹ (lô) "to him" לֹא (lo') "not" Ps. 100:3; compare NIV and NASB
Homoeoteleuton	Two lines end in the same word resulting in the scribe's skipping a line	Judg. 16:13-14 1 Sam. 14:41
Haplography	Letters written once instead of twice	Judg. 20:13 "sons" is missing בני בנימן
Dittography	Letters written twice instead of once	Ezek. 16:6 (Hebrew and NASB)
Word division	Words divided incorrectly	Hos. 6:5
Letter metathesis	Letters mistakenly reversed make a different word	Ps. 49:11 (Heb. 12) קרב or קבר
Marginalia	Words mistakenly inserted from margin to text or inserted in an incorrect position	Isa. 38:21-22 in wrong place (cf. 2 Kings 20:7-8) Josh. 2:15 (second part of verse absent from Septuagint)

Old Testament
Textual Development

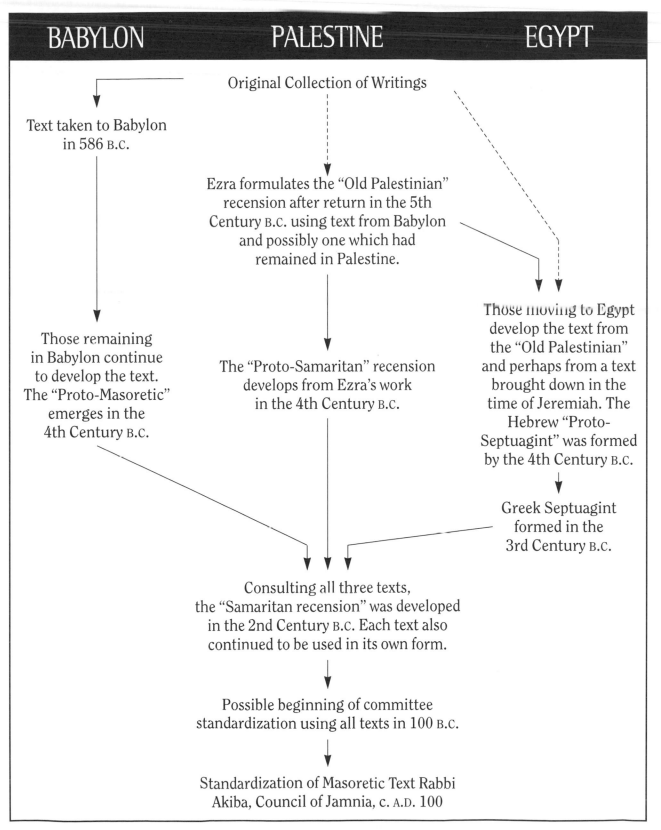

BABYLON	PALESTINE	EGYPT

Original Collection of Writings

Text taken to Babylon in 586 B.C.

Ezra formulates the "Old Palestinian" recension after return in the 5th Century B.C. using text from Babylon and possibly one which had remained in Palestine.

Those moving to Egypt develop the text from the "Old Palestinian" and perhaps from a text brought down in the time of Jeremiah. The Hebrew "Proto-Septuagint" was formed by the 4th Century B.C.

Those remaining in Babylon continue to develop the text. The "Proto-Masoretic" emerges in the 4th Century B.C.

The "Proto-Samaritan" recension develops from Ezra's work in the 4th Century B.C.

Greek Septuagint formed in the 3rd Century B.C.

Consulting all three texts, the "Samaritan recension" was developed in the 2nd Century B.C. Each text also continued to be used in its own form.

Possible beginning of committee standardization using all texts in 100 B.C.

Standardization of Masoretic Text Rabbi Akiba, Council of Jamnia, c. A.D. 100

Most of this material is highly theoretical, but it is backed by some evidence.

Principles for Word Studies

PRINCIPLE	ENGLISH EXAMPLE	OT EXAMPLE FOR ENGLISH READER	OT EXAMPLE FOR HEBREW STUDENT
Verbs and nouns that share the same root do not always share the same semantic meaning.	Verb: to undertake Noun: undertaker	A noun's meaning (e.g., #6625, *almah*) cannot be deduced from its verbal root (#6623, *'alam*).	מִדְבָּר (wilderness) has no connection in meaning to the verb דבר; also עָלְמָה and עלם.
The various stems of a particular verbal root are not necessarily related in meaning.	No equivalent situation for verbs, but with nouns "adult" and "adultery"	NIV concordance usually separates, e.g., #4106 and #4105; see also #3877 and 3878.	כפר in the qal (G) is "to cover" and is unrelated to כֹּפֶר in the piel (D), usually translated "to atone."
One must consider whether verb + preposition combinations take on special meanings.	Verb alone: To believe someone Verb + preposition: to believe in someone	Difficult to separate contexts with English helps; NIV combines in one entry, see #2047.	הגה with no preposition means to ponder action; with בּ = meditate; with כּ = animal sounds; with לּ = desire.
Meanings attached to a word in an idiomatic expression cannot necessarily be attached to that word outside of that expression.	"Just a minute" as an idiomatic expression refers to an undefined period of time. This meaning could not be applied to other contexts, e.g., class will be 50 minutes long.	NIV concordance often lists idiomatic phrases separately, see entry #3427 "day." Meaning found in one idiom cannot be transferred automatically to other idioms or usages.	In the phrase "Day of the Lord" יוֹם does not refer to a 24-hour period; this meaning of יוֹם cannot be applied to other contexts because it is dependent on the idiomatic phrase.
When it is established that several different meanings exist for a word, the interpreter still must seek clues from the context as to which meaning the author intended.	"Minutes" can mean parts of an hour or notes of meeting decisions. In the ambiguous sentence "Additional minutes are available on request," the hearer must discern which the speaker meant.	The list of translations in e.g., #8120, cannot be used as a menu from which the interpreter may select any entry for use in any occurrence of the word.	רוּחַ can mean either wind or spirit. The interpreter is not therefore at liberty to choose whichever meaning he wants in a given context, but must determine which the author intended.

6625 עַלְמָה *'almāh* (7)
maiden (2)
maidens (2)
girl (1)
virgin (1)
virgins (1)

6623 עָלַם *'ālam* (29)
hidden (4)
ignore (4)
unaware of (3) +4946
hard (2)
hide (2)
bring (1)
close (1)
close (1) +6623
closes (1)
hiding (1)
hypocrites (1)
make shut (1)
obscures (1)
secret (1)
shut (1)

swollen (1)
turn away (1)
unaware (1) +4946+6524

2047 הָגָה 1 *hāgāh1* (25)
meditate (3)
plot (3)
growls (1)
lament (1)
meditates (1)
moan (1)
moan mournfully (1) +2047
moaned (1)
mutter (1)
mutters (1)
ponder (1)
speak (1)
speaks (1)
tell (1)
think (1)
utter (1)
utter a sound (1)
uttering (1)

utters (1)
weighs (1)

4105 1 כָּפַר *kāpar1* (101)
make atonement (58)
making atonement (6)
atonement made (5)
made atonement (4)
atone (3)
be atoned for (3)
forgave (2)
forgive (2)
makes atonement (2)
accept atonement (1)
appease (1)
atoned for (1)
atonement (1)
atonement be made (1)
atonement made (1) +4113
atonement was made (1)
be annulled (1)
be atoned (1)
is atoned for (1)

make amends (1)
pacify (1) +7156
pardon (1)
ward off with a ransom (1)
untranslated (2)

4106 2 כָּפַר *kāpar2* (1)
coat (1)

8120 רוּחַ *rûah* (379)
spirit (176)
wind (79)
breath (31)
winds (13)
mind (5)
heart (4)
side (4)
spirits (4)
blast (3)
sides (3)
anger (2)
courage (2)
feelings (2)

Note: Numbers in column 3 are from John R. Kohlenberger III and Edward W. Goodrick, *The NIV Exhaustive Concordance* (Grand Rapids: Zondervan, 1990).

Principles for Word Studies

PRINCIPLE	ENGLISH EXAMPLE	OT EXAMPLE FOR ENGLISH READER	OT EXAMPLE FOR HEBREW STUDENT
The original meaning (etymology) of a word is an unreliable guide to its current usage.	Originally "awful" meant full of awe, but that gives no indication of modern usage.	NIV concordance usually keeps such entries separate, e.g., #2417 and 2416. Students should not ignore these distinctions.	זָקֵן, beard was originally related to the idea of being old (see verb and adj.), but that gives no indication of its usage.
Similar (cognate) vocabulary from other related languages is an unreliable guide to meaning.	One cannot determine the meaning of "dynamite" by its Greek cognate, *Dunamos* (=power).	#9592, *tᵉšûqāh*, the commentators often attach a particular nuance based on Arabic etymology.	The meaning of תְּשׁוּקָה e.g. in Gen. 3:16; 4:7 cannot be determined reliably from Arabic usage.
To understand the importance of a particular word usage in context, one must know what choices (synonyms) were available, and what is signified by the choice that was made.	If one reads "mustang," one can draw certain conclusions because the author did not use stallion, mare, steed, or charger.	In an entry such as "girl" (NIV concordance p. 416) the fact that #1435, 5855 and 6625 all occur does not mean they all mean the same.	The nouns בְּתוּלָה, עַלְמָה and נַעֲרָה overlap in meaning, but each has its own semantic range. The interpreter must determine the unique domain of each.
When a word has a technical sense and general sense, context must be used to determine which was intended.	"Reformed" can be used in a general sense or can refer to a theological system.	Since #8477 lists technical as well as general meanings, some of the passages listed under "Satan" on p. 989 may be subject to reconsideration.	שָׂטָן may refer to a human (1 Kgs 11:23) or to the Angel of the Lord (Num 22:22). Translation as Satan must be defended from context.
Meaning must be construed in a broad enough sense to suit all appropriate contexts (this would *not* include idiomatic or technical usages).	The verb "to swim" could not be defined by a particular arm stroke for many different types of strokes can be used.	If a particular nuance is suggested for #1343, *bara'*, each of the relevant occurrences listed in 1343 should be checked.	בָּרָא cannot mean creation out of nothing, or it could not be used in Gen. 5:1. Gen 2:7 shows that man was not created out of nothing.

2416 זָקֵן *zāqēn1* (26)
Old (22)
aged (1) +4394
grew old (1)
grew old (1)
very old (1) +928+995+2021+3427

2417 זָקֵן *zāqēn1* (19)
beard (11)
beards (5)
chin (2)
hair (1)

9592 תְּשׁוּקָה *tᵉšûqāh* (3)
desire (2)
desires (1)

1343 בָּרָא *bārā'1* (48)
created (210)
create (10)
were created (6)
creator (3)
are created (2)
creating (2)
brings about (1)
creates (1)
done (1)
not yet created (1)

GIRL (57) [GIRL'S, GIRLS]

Ge	24:14	May it be that when I say to a g.	5855
	24:16	The g was very beutiful, a virgin;	5855
	24:28	The g ran and told her mother's household	5855
	24:55	"Let the g ramain with us ten days or so;	5855
	24:57	"Let's call the g and ask her about it."	5855
	29:24	And Laban gave his servant g Zilpah	9148
	29:29	Laban gave his servant g Bilhah	9148
	34: 3	he loved the g and spoke tenderly to her.	5855
	34: 4	"Get me this g as my wife."	3530
	34:12	Only give me the g as my wife."	5855
Ex	1:16	but if it is a g, let her live.	1426
	1:22	but let every g live	1426
	2: 5	the reeds and sent her slave g to get it.	563
	2: 8	and the g went and got the baby's mother.	6625
Lev	11: 5	to the firstborn son of the slave g,	9148
	12: 7	the woman who gives birth to a boy or a g.	5922
	19:20	with a woman who is a slave g promised	9148
Nu	31:18	every g who has never slept with a man	851+3251
Dt	22:24	the g because she was in a town and did	5855
	22:25	a g pledged to be married and rapes her.	5855
	22:26	Do nothing to the g;	5855
	22:27	for the man found **the** g out in the country.	2023ˢ
	22:27	and though the betrothed g screamed	5855
	22:29	He must marry the g,	NIH
Jdg	5:30	a g or two for each man,	8167
	9:18	the sone of his **slave** g,	563
1Sa	30:19	young or old, boy or g.	1426
2Sa	17:17	A **servant** g was to go and inform them,	9148
1Ki	1: 3	for a beautiful g and found Abishag,	5855
	1: 4	The g was very beautiful;	5855
2Ki	5: 2	and had taken captive a young g	5855
	5: 4	to his master and told him what the g	5855
Est	2: 4	the g who pleases the king be queen instead	5855
	2: 7	This g, who was also known as Esther,	5855

	2: 9	This g pleased him and won his favor.	5855
	2:15	for Esther (**the** g Mordecai had adopted.	889ˢ
Job	31: 1	with my eyes not to look lustfully at a g.	1435
Am	2: 7	the same g and so profane my holy name.	5855

8477 שָׂטָן *śāṭān* (27)
Satan (18)
adversary (4)
oppose (2)
accuser (1)
adversaries (1)
turn against (1) +2118+4200

SATAN (53) [SATAN'S]

1Ch	21: 1	S rose up against Israel and incited David	8477
Job	1: 6	and S also came with them.	8477
	1: 7	The LORD said to S, "Where have you come	8477
	1: 7	S answered the Lord, "From roaming	8477
	1: 8	the LORD said to S, "Have you considered	8477
	1: 9	Job fear God for nothing?" S replied.	8477
	1:12	The Lord said to S, "Very well, then,	8477
	1:12	Then S went out from the presence of	8477
	2: 1	and S also came with them	8477
	2: 2	the Lord said to S, "where have you come	8477
	2: 2	S answered the LORD, "from roaming	8477
	2: 3	the LORD said to S, "where have you come	8477
	2: 4	"Skin for skin!" S replied.	8477
	2: 6	The LORD said to S, "Very well, then,	8477
	2: 7	So S went out from the presence of	8477
Zec	3: 1	S standing at his right side to accuse him.	8477
	3: 2	The LORD said to S, The LORD rebuke you,	8477
	3: 2	The LORD rebuke you, S!	8477

Forms of Critical Analysis

Textual Criticism	What words were in the original text?
Linguistic Criticism	What do the words and phrases mean?
Literary Criticism	What are the circumstances of the literature? (author, date, place, audience, sources, purpose)
Form Criticism	What is the literary (oral or written) genre of each of the parts? What brought about the existence of this genre? (*sitz im leben*)
Historical Criticism	What is the historical setting that brought about this piece of literature?
Redaction Criticism	How was the literary work compiled and to what purpose? What is the theological role intended for the text?
Tradition Criticism	What are the stages through which a piece of literature evolved and grew?
Canonical Criticism	What function was served by the final form of the canonical literature within the religious community?

Creation Theories

THEORY	DESCRIPTION	UNDERSTANDING OF TIME	TREATMENT OF "DAY"	MAJOR PROBLEMS
24-HOUR DAY	Views chapter 1 as sequential and literal	Most support "young earth"	24 hours	• Reconciling with scientific data • Integrating chapters 1 & 2
DAY-AGE	Views creation as taking place over six eras	Unlimited time available for each era	Day = age	• Sequence still does not suit scientific data • Difficult to substantiate author's intention as day = age • Often an excuse for evolution
LITERARY APPROACH	Views seven-day sequence as a literary structure	Narrative has nothing to say about time	Oriented toward sabbath theology	• Exodus 20:11 • Difficult to preclude time significance only on basis of literary structure
PRIOR CREATION	Suggests existence of a previous created world prior to Genesis 1	Most of scientific ages related to prior creation	24 hours	• No textual support • Questions of continuity in scientific record • Sun/moon
TWO-PHASE	Two distinct phases of creation in chapters 1 & 2 with long period of time in between	Gap between 2:3 and 2:4 can accommodate any time requirements	Any view possible	• People in chapter 1 are not Adam and Eve and must be viewed as not yet morally responsible

Identity of the "Sons of God"
Genesis 6:1-2

	MATERIAL DISTINCTION	THEOLOGICAL DISTINCTION	SOCIAL DISTINCTION	NO DISTINCTION
SONS OF GOD	Fallen angels	Godly line of Seth	Dynastic rulers	Royal heroes of old
DAUGHTERS OF MEN	Mortals	Line of Cain	Commoners	Any woman
OFFENSE	Marriage between supernatural and mortal	Marriage of holy to unholy	Polygamy	Right of the first night: king, acting in place of deity, could spend first night with any woman getting married (fertility rite)
EVIDENCE	1. The term "sons of God" refers only to angels. (Job 1; 38:7; Ps. 29:1; 89:7) 2. Jude 6-7 perhaps refers to this incident. (See also 2 Peter 2:4) 3. It is the clear reading of the text 4. The Septuagint in Job 1 reads "angels of God" 5. Christ says angels do not marry; doesn't say "cannot"	1. The concept of a holy line is seemingly established (Gen. 4:26) 2. Hebrew indicates continuity from the previous chapter 3. The sin here becomes a common theme throughout the Pentateuch	1. Magistrates or rulers often referred to as gods (Exod. 21:6; 22:8, 9, 28; Ps. 82:1, 6) 2. Kings sometimes called sons of deities (2 Sam. 7:14)	1. Ancient kings were regularly portrayed as sons of God 2. Practice attested in Gilgamesh Epic (Ps. 4:32-4) as offensive 3. Matches language of text: took wives, whichever they chose
PROBLEMS	1. Lends mythological tone 2. Angels were not previously mentioned 3. Why is man punished by the Flood for the wickedness of angels? 4. New Testament support is questionable	1. The term "sons of God" never means this elsewhere 2. No evidence that the lines are kept totally separate. The theory does not account for Adam and Eve's other children 3. God has not yet begun working through one line. (No concept of election) 4. The term for men is general. It would need further classification to be understood otherwise 5. In Noah's time he alone was holy	1. Kingship is not expressed in any way 2. Scripture never speaks of kings in a group as sons of deity 3. Needs the connection of v. 4, but the "mighty men" are the Nephilim, not the children of the union	1. Scripture never speaks of kings in a group as sons of deity 2. "Right of the first night" is not widely attested in Ancient Near East

For a full discussion see *The Genesis Debate*, ed. Ronald Youngblood (Grand Rapids: Baker, 1990), 184-209.

Comparison of Chronological Systems

EARLY EXODUS LONG SOJOURN	EARLY EXODUS SHORT SOJOURN	LATE EXODUS	RECONSTRUCTIONIST

		2100		

The Patriarchs
2166-1805

Migration to Egypt 1876

2000

1900

The Patriarchs
1952-1589

Migration to
Egypt 1660

The Patriarchs
1950-1650

Migration to
Egypt 1650

1800

Egyptian sojourn
1876-1446

Slavery
1730 or 1580

1700

Egyptian sojourn
1660-1446
Slavery 1580

1600

1500

Egyptian sojourn
1650-1230

Slavery 1580

The Patriarchs
1500-1300

Gradual migration

Egyptian sojourn
1350-1230

1400

Wandering
1446-1406

Conquest and judges
1406-1050

Wandering
1446-1406

Conquest and judges
1406-1050

1300

1200

Conquest and judges
1230-1025

Conquest and judges
1230-1025

1100

United Kingdom
1050-931

United Kingdom
1050-931

1000

United Kingdom
1025-931

United Kingdom
1025-931

900

Early date for Exodus and 430-year sojourn in Egypt per Masoretic reading of Exod. 12:40	Early date of Exodus and 215-year sojourn in Egypt per LXX reading of Exod. 12:40	Late date of Exodus and belief in historicity of patriarchal events	Late date of Exodus and reconstruction of biblical history through use of form criticism

Extent of the Flood:
Part 1

UNIVERSAL FLOOD: EVIDENCE	LOCAL FLOOD: REBUTTAL
The language of the account over and over expresses totality (Gen. 7:18-24).	The account is from the viewpoint of the narrator, and from his perspective it is total. "All" doesn't always mean "all" (Gen. 41:57; Deut. 2:25; 1 Kings 18:10).
If 150 days were needed for the water to recede, it must have been universal.	A large-scale local flood could take that long and, even with wind drying it, a universal flood would take much longer.
The size of the ark indicates that this was no local flood.	A large ark was needed because of the number of animals it had to house; the size is not related to the extent of the flood.
If the flood was only local, why was the ark necessary at all?	That is the way God chose to save. Building the ark gave Noah an opportunity to preach.
The purpose of the flood was the punishment of worldwide sin. A local flood would not do; some could have escaped.	God could have made certain all flesh was destroyed without flooding the entire globe.
There are universal traditions of people with accounts of a flood.	Many don't have the tradition (e.g., Egypt); many accounts do not claim the flood was universal; there are many differences in the various accounts.
There are world-wide traces of the flood. A universal flood is geologically supportable.	Evidence is scattered, inconsistent, and unsubstantial. There is no conclusive geologic evidence for such a catastrophe.
The promise of no future floods (Gen. 9:15) would be false if it had been only a local flood.	Though local, it still could have been greater than any since. Also, the promise is for no flood "to destroy all flesh"; intent is stressed.
A universal flood is the clearest meaning of the text and has priority.	Scientific evidence against universal flood is of such an extent that secondary reading of the text is necessary.
Ending ice ages, dissolving canopies, continental drifting, and/or changes in the angle of the earth were all used to create necessary conditions.	This argument is too theoretical and perhaps these phenomena would still be insufficient. Also, they do not explain everything.
The mountains of Ararat are high and since water seeks its own level and the ark came to rest there, they must have been covered.	The ark did not land on a peak of the mountain, but somewhere in that chain. Noah and his family could not possibly have gotten down from a peak.

Note: The evidence and rebuttals presented are not purported by their mere presentation to be scientifically accurate. We are unqualified to make that judgment. The chart only represents the arguments on each side, not a certification of their factuality. The major sources are J. Whitcomb and

Extent of the Flood:
Part II

LOCAL FLOOD: EVIDENCE	UNIVERSAL FLOOD: REBUTTAL
A local flood is indicated by the fact that the ark came to rest within 500 miles of its starting point.	God's guiding hand has accomplished things more remarkable.
To flood the entire globe would need 8 times the amount of water now available in our system. No miracle is mentioned. Where did it come from?	It came from an atmospheric source (canopy theory), but not that much was needed because the land was much lower, mountains were raised after flood.
Mixing of fresh and salt water would be disastrous for fish.	We don't know the adaptability of fish at that time, but even if most were destroyed, God could easily have preserved 2 of each species.
If 8 times our present amount of water rained down, there would have been a detectable dilution of salt waters.	The earth had much less water in its system before the flood, and salt water was much lower in saline content. Salt content would quickly equalize.
The amount of water required for a universal flood would have totally destroyed most plant life.	Enough plant life would have survived by floating and by preserved seeds.
There would be great difficulty not only in storing enough food, but in the actual caring for the animals.	It is suggested that most, if not all, of the animals hibernated to some extent.
The biblical record concerns itself only with those peoples interacting with Israel. Other lands were not involved.	The biblical record implies that the earth was populated by the descendants of Noah (see also Luke 17:26-30 and 2 Peter 2:5).
Noah did not go to Africa, China, etc., to preach repentance. The tone of the passage is local.	We are nowhere told that Noah spoke to everyone affected by the flood. Noah alone found favor in the eyes of the Lord.
The fossil sequence in geologic strata worldwide show little variation from what would be expected. A universal flood would have caused hopeless shuffling.	The sequence is often reversed. Also, fossil sequencing is based on the evolutionary model, which is here rejected.

101

H. M. Morris, *The Genesis Flood* (Nutley, N.J.: Presbyterian and Reformed, 1960); B. Ramm, *The Christian View of Science and Scripture* (Grand Rapids: Eerdmans, 1954); W. Ault, "The Flood," in *The Zondervan Pictorial Encyclopedia of the Bible* (Grand Rapids: Zondervan, 1975).

Date of the Exodus:
Part 1

15th-CENTURY EVIDENCE	13th-CENTURY REBUTTAL
I Kings 6:1 designates 480 years from the Exodus to Solomon's dedication of the temple. The dedication was 966. That makes the Exodus 1446.	The 480 years is most likely 12 generations (12x40=480). In actuality, a generation was about 25 years, making the actual figure about 300.
The "Dream Stela" of Thutmose IV on the sphinx gives evidence that Thutmose was not legal heir to the throne. Would be logical that eldest son was killed in the 10th plague.	Only one of many other possibilities. No proof that the biblical plague was involved in the death of the rightful heir.
In Judges 11:26, Jephthah assigns 300 years between his day (c. 1100) and the Conquest. This would seem to indicate a 15th-century Exodus.	This was a generalization or a rough and slightly inaccurate guess by Jephthah who would have had no access to historical records.
To support the biblical chronology of Moses, Pharaoh must have reigned in excess of 40 years. Moses stayed in the wilderness until Pharaoh died. Only possibilities: Thutmose III, Rameses II.	Moses' 40 years with the Midianites is not really a chronological reference.
The Last Level at Hazor, wiped out by Barak and Deborah, contains Mycenaean IIIB Pottery; this requires, at the latest, a date in the late 13th century. This pushes Exodus much earlier.	The judges overlapped enough to accommodate this.
The Merneptah Stela (C. 1220) mentions Israel by name. They must have been there for a long time for the Egyptians to accept them as a nation.	Fifty years would have been sufficient time.
The Amarna Tablets (1400) tell of the upheaval caused by the "Habiru." This could have been the Hebrews, possibly classified under a general category.	The "Habiru" can in no way be identified with the Israelites.
The length of time assigned to the judges period in Scripture, even with overlapping, cannot be squeezed into the century and a half allowed by a 13th-century Exodus.	With overlaps and understanding of the symbolic nature of time spans, it can be fitted in.

Date of the Exodus:
Part II

13th-CENTURY EVIDENCE	15th-CENTURY REBUTTAL
The civilizations of Edom, Moab, and Ammon were not in existence in the 15th century. Since Israel had contact with them, the Exodus must be later.	Finds at the Timna temple indicate sedentary civilizations in Negev at least in early 14th century. Tribes were wandering earlier than that.
The destruction of Lachish, Debir, and Bethel were in the 13th century, as indicated by the layer of ash.	Lachish, Debir, and Bethel are not said to have been burned at the time of the Conquest. The layer of ash could be due to Egypt's conquests.
In Exodus 1:11, Israelites were said to have been building the city of Rameses. This must be in honor of Rameses II of 13th century.	(1) Name "Rameses" used much earlier than 13th century. (2) City was being built before birth of Moses; thus, before Rameses II, even with late Exodus. (3) This was a store city, not a capital.
The 430 years of Exodus 12:40 cannot fit in with the Hyksos period.	The Hebrews need not be related to the Hyksos. There is much evidence that Jacob went to Egypt almost 150 years before the Hyksos period began.
Thutmose III was not known as a great builder and therefore does not fit into the historical picture.	Though not known as a great builder, Thutmose III is known to have had some building projects in the delta region.
Scripture does not mention the Palestinian invasions of Seti I or Rameses II. Therefore, Exodus must have been in 13th century and Israel was not yet in Palestine.	It is very likely that the periods of "rest" during the Judges were the periods of tighter Egyptian control. The Egyptian invasions were against the Canaanites.
Pushing the Exodus back means pushing the patriarchs back, and the Patriarchs cannot go back any farther.	There is just as much evidence for putting the patriarchs in Middle Bronze I as there is for putting them in Middle Bronze II.

Views Concerning the Fate of Jephthah's Daughter

DEDICATED	SACRIFICED
1. Being a judge, Jephthah must have been God-fearing, so he would not have violated Law	**1. Promise of a simple animal sacrifice would hardly be a convincing vow in this situation**
2. The Spirit of the Lord comes on Jephthah and he is mentioned in Heb. 11 so he would not have violated Law	2. The mention of something coming out of the house implies that human sacrifice was intended
3. Daughter bewails her virginity and 11:39 makes comment that "she knew not a man"	**3. The burnt offering ('olah) involves death in all 286 O.T. occurrences**
4. Evidence of women in service of tabernacle—Ex. 38:8; I Sam. 2:22	4. If it was frequent practice to have women enter tabernacle service, why the commemoration?
5. Human sacrifice would have been clearly understood as a violation of God's Law, and public opinion would have disallowed it even if Jephthah wanted to proceed	**5. Human sacrifice is seen as a last ditch effort in battle (2 Kings 3:27)**
6. Lev. 27:1-8 allows for redemption of humans vowed for sacrifice	6. The conjunction in 11:31 is one of apposition: "will be the Lord's, that is I will sacrifice it as a burnt offering"
7. The conjunction in 11:31 should be rendered or, showing Jephthah considered various situations	**7. There is little evidence of Jephthah's spirituality or knowledge of the Law**

Views Concerning Daniel's Four Empires

NEBUCHADNEZZAR'S DREAM STATUE (Dan. 2)	DANIEL'S VISION OF BEASTS (Dan. 7)	POSITION #1	POSITION #2	POSITION #3
HEAD GOLD	Lion with eagle wings	BABYLON	BABYLON	Nebuchadnezzar (2:38)
CHEST SILVER	Bear	MEDIA	MEDO-PERSIA	MEDIA Contemporaneous to Nebuchadnezzar's successors
	3 Ribs in mouth	Darius the Mede —considered historically inaccurate	3 Ribs = Lydia, Babylon, and Egypt	3 Ribs = Urartu, Scythia, and Mannaeans (cf. Jer. 51:27-29)
	Leopard with	PERSIA	GREEK	PERSIA
TORSO BRONZE	4 wings and 4 heads	First 4 Persian kings or 4 directions	4 generals who divide up Alexander's Empire	First 4 kings of Persia (Dan. 11:2)
	Unnamed beast	GREECE	ROMAN	GREECE
LEGS IRON, FEET IRON and POTTERY	10 horns	10 horns = Seleucid kings Little horn = Antichus IV Epiphanes	3 options: Past fulfillment Future fulfillment in extended empire Future fulfillment in reconstituted empire	10 Horns = Ten sovereign states that had grown out of Alexander's empire by the 2nd c. B.C.

Views Concerning Daniel's 70 Weeks

ISSUES	MACCABEAN	ROMAN	ESCHATOLOGICAL			
			I - SYMBOLIC		II - INTERVAL	
			Decree of Cyrus	Jeremiah's prophetic word 594	One of the decrees of Artaxerxes 458 or 445	
Beginning point (Decree, v. 25)	605/586 Beginning of Captivity	Variously one of 3 Persian Decrees 538, 458, 445				
Messiah the Prince v. 25	Cyrus	Jesus	Jesus	Cyrus	Jesus	
62 Weeks	538-170 Cyrus - Antiochus IV Epiphanes	Added to 7 weeks to span from decree to point in life of Christ	Church Age	Indefinite period from Cyrus until end	Added to 7 weeks and by using "prophetic years" ends at triumphal entry	
Messiah v. 26	Onias III High Priest murdered 171 B.C.	Jesus	Jesus at Tribulation	Antichrist	Jesus at Crucifixion	
Covenant - Maker v. 27	Antiochus IV Epiphanes with renegade Jews	Jesus	Antichrist	Antichrist	Antichrist	
70th Week	Persecution of Antiochus IV Epiphanes 171-164	Roman destruction of Jerusalem by Titus, 70 A.D.	Tribulation	Tribulation	Tribulation	

Messiah in the Old Testament

High Priest	Lev. 4:3, 5, 16 Lev. 5:15

Specific Kings of Israel	Saul (11x: 1 Sam. 12: 3, 5; 24:6, 7, 10;
	    26:9, 11, 16, 23; 2 Sam. 1:14, 16)
	David (7x: 2 Sam. 19:21; 22:51; 23:21;
	    Pss. 18:50; 20:6; 28:8; 132:17)
	Solomon (2 Chr. 6:42)
	Zedekiah ? (Lam. 4:20)

Other specified individuals	The Patriarchs (1 Chr. 16:22/ Ps. 105:15) Cyrus (Isa. 45:1) Eliab (1 Sam. 16:6)
General references to King of Israel (usually Davidic; could be present, future or ideal)	Hab. 3:13 1 Sam. 2:10 (Hannah's song) 1 Sam. 2:35 Pss. 2:2; 84:9; 89:38, 51; 132:10
Indefinite reference to future, unidentified individual	Dan. 9:25-26

The Angel of the Lord in the Old Testament

Informing those chosen for leadership	Moses (Ex. 3) Gideon (Judg. 6) Samson's Parents (Judg. 13) Joshua the High Priest (Zech. 3)
Providing Instruction to Prophets	Balaam (Num. 22) Elijah (2 Kings 1)
Providing Specific Instruction to Individuals	Hagar (Gen. 16; 21) Abraham (Gen. 22:11, 15) Jacob (Gen. 31:11)
Pronouncing Judgment	Judg. 2: 1-4 Judg. 5:23
Carrying Out Judgment/ Providing Protection	Red Sea (Ex. 14) Ps. 34:7 David's Census (2 Sam. 24 = 1 Chr. 21) Sennacherib's Army (2 Kings 19:35 = Isa. 37:36)
Interceding on behalf of Israel	Zechariah's first vision (Zech. 1:11-12)
Observations	People can be referred to as the Angel (messenger) of the Lord (Hag. 1:13; Mal. 2:7) The Angel of the Lord can also be referred to as the Angel of God (Judg. 13)

Satan in the Old Testament

1. Verb

"to oppose as an adversary"

Psalm 71:13
Psalm 109:4, 20, 29
Psalm 38:20
Zechariah 3:1

2. Noun

Human beings ("adversary")

1 Samuel 29:4 (David to the Philistines)
2 Samuel 19:23 (Abishai to David)
1 Kings 5:4
1 Kings 11:14 (Hadad to Solomon)
1 Kings 11:23 (Rezon to Solomon)
1 Kings 11:25 (Rezon to Solomon)
Psalm 109:6

Supernatural beings

With the definite article (use of the definite article suggests that the author was using it as a function rather than as a personal name (i.e., "the adversary" rather than "Satan")

14 times in Job 1-2
3 times in Zechariah 3:1-2

Without the definite article (could indicate either a personal name or an adversary not specifically known or identified)

Numbers 22:22, 32 (Angel of the Lord to Balaam)
1 Chronicles 21:1

The Ark of the Covenant
Footstool of the Lord
(1 Chron. 28:2; Ps. 132:7-8; cf. 99:5)

Construction	Instructions (Exod. 25:10-22) Craftsmen: Bezalel and Oholiab (Exod. 31:1-7) Specifications: acacia wood overlaid with gold; ca. 4' x 2' x 2' (Exod. 37:1-9) Furnishing of Tabernacle (Exod. 39:35) Covered by shielding curtain (Exod. 40:21) and sea cow hides and blue cloth (Num. 4:4-6)
Premonarchy Period	Tablets of the Law inside (Deut. 10:5) (and jar of Manna and Aaron's rod that budded according to Heb. 9:4; cf. Exod. 16:32-4; Num. 17:8-10) Levites care for it (Deut. 10:8) Led Israel into Canaan (Josh. 3:10-11) Parting of the Jordan (Josh. 3:13-17) Battle of Jericho (Josh. 6:8-14) Residing at Bethel (Judg. 20:27) Residing at Shiloh (1 Sam. 1-3) Taken into the Battle of Ebenezer by Eli's sons (1 Sam. 4:1-5)
Ark in Exile	Captured by the Philistines (1 Sam. 4:11) Placed in Philistine temple at the feet of Dagon (1 Sam. 5:2) Idol of Dagon humiliated (1 Sam. 5:3-5) Brought plagues on Philistines (1 Sam. 5:6) Ark returned to Israel after 7 months (1 Sam. 6:1-12) Residents of Beth-Shemesh struck down for looking inside (1 Sam. 6:19) Residing at Kiriath-jearim at the house of Abinidab (20 years; 1 Sam. 7:1-2) Neglected during the reign of Saul (1 Chron. 13:3)
Monarchy in Jerusalem	Brought from Kiriath-jearim (2 Sam. 6:2) Uzzah struck down for mishandling (2 Sam. 6:6-7) Residing at the home of Obed-Edom the Gittite (3 months; 2 Sam. 6:10-11) Brought to Jerusalem (2 Sam. 6:12-17) Taken into battle at seige of Rabbah (2 Sam. 11:11) Initially brought with David into exile, but returned (2 Sam. 15:24-25) Brought into Solomon's Temple (1 Kings 8:3-8) Still in Jerusalem at end of 7th century (2 Chron. 35:3; Jer 3:16) Most likely taken by Babylonians in 586 (2 Esdras 10:20-23) Absent from Ezekiel's Temple Vision (Ezek. 40-48) Not rebuilt for second temple (Josephus, *Jewish Wars* 1:152-3; 5:5)

"And the Spirit of the Lord Came Upon Them"

	PERSON	REFERENCE
SKILL	Bezalel	Exodus 31:3; 35:30-31
LEADERSHIP	Moses	Numbers 11:17
	Joshua	Deuteronomy 34:9
	Othniel	Judges 3:10
	Gideon	Judges 6:34
	Jephthah	Judges 11:29
	Samson	Judges 14:6, 19; 15:14
	David	1 Samuel 16:13
	Saul	1 Samuel 10:10; 11:6; 19:23
PROPHECY	Seventy Elders	Numbers 11:25
	Balaam	Numbers 24:2
	Messengers of Saul	1 Samuel 19:20
	Amasa	1 Chronicles 12:18
	Azarash	2 Chronicles 15:1
	Zechariah	2 Chronicles 24:20
	Isaiah	Isaiah 61:1
	Ezekiel	Ezekiel 3:24; 11:15

Dreams and Visions

	REFERENCE	SUBJECT	DREAM OR VISION	REFERENCE	SUBJECT	DREAM OR VISION
PENTATEUCH	Gen. 15	Abraham	The Lord passing between the pieces. Confirmation of covenant	Gen. 37	Joseph	Sheaves and stars bowing down
	Gen. 20	Abimelech of Gerar	The Lord's warning concerning Sarah	Gen. 40	Chief butler	Himself squeezing grapes into Pharaoh's cup
	Gen. 28	Jacob	Ladder to heaven with angels ascending and descending	Gen. 40	Chief baker	Himself carrying baskets of bread and birds eating from them
	Gen. 31:1-13	Jacob	God telling Jacob to leave land and return to Israel	Gen. 41	Pharaoh	Fat cows devoured by thin cows; plump ears of corn eaten by thin ears
	Gen. 31:24	Laban	God telling Laban not to harm Jacob	Gen. 46:2-4	Jacob	God telling Jacob to go to Egypt
MAJOR PROPHETS	Isa. 6	Isaiah	The Lord and the Seraphim in the temple	Ezek. 40-48	Ezekiel	Man showing the temple
	Jer. 1	Jeremiah	Almond tree, boiling pot	Dan. 2	Nebuchad-nezzar	Colossus figure of 4 metals
	Jer. 24	Jeremiah	2 baskets of figs	Dan. 4	Nebuchad-nezzar	Chopping down of the tree
	Ezek. 1	Ezekiel	4 living beings; gleaming wheels; glory of the Lord	Dan. 7	Daniel	4 Beasts, 10 Horns
	Ezek. 8-9	Ezekiel	Slaying of the guilty	Dan. 8	Daniel	Ram, male goat
	Ezek. 10-11	Ezekiel	Whirling wheels; cherubim	Dan. 10-12	Daniel	Angel telling of latter days
	Ezek. 37	Ezekiel	Valley of dry bones	Dan. 2:19	Daniel	Interpretation of Nebuchadnezzar's dream
MINOR PROPHETS	Amos 7	Amos	Locust swarm; fire; plumb line	Zech. 3	Zechariah	Joshua given clean garments
	Amos 8	Amos	Summer fruit	Zech. 4	Zechariah	Lampstand and two olive trees
	Zech. 1	Zechariah	Different-colored horses and patrol riders	Zech. 5	Zechariah	Flying scroll
	Zech. 1	Zechariah	4 horns; 4 craftsmen	Zech. 5	Zechariah	Woman in ephah
	Zech. 2	Zechariah	Man with measuring line	Zech. 6	Zechariah	4 chariots with different-colored horses
HIST.	Judg. 7:13-15	Midianite	Loaf of barley fore-telling Gideon's victory	1 Kings 3:5-15	Solomon	The Lord's offer to Solomon

112

Note; Other instances mentioned as visions are oracles of some sort consisting primarily of a spoken message.
Cf. Isa. 1:1; Obad. 1; Nahum 1:1; Hab. 2:2; 1 Chron. 17:3-15; 2 Sam. 7:3-17.

The People of God and the Covenant

PEOPLE OF GOD	ISRAEL: Medium of REVELATION						CHURCH: Heirs of SALVATION
						EVENTS SURROUNDING RETURN END REVELATORY FUNCTION. FOCUS TURNS TO REMNANT	Christ and Church
History	Patriarchal Period	First Transitionary Period: Egyptian Sojourn	Conquest and Judges	Second Transitionary Period: Ark in Exile (1 Sam. 4-2 Sam. 6)	Monarchy	Third Transitionary Period: Exile, Post-Exilic and Intertestamental Periods / Daniel's 4 Kingdoms	
The Covenant	Promises to Abraham (initiation of the covenant)						
LAND							
NATION							
BLESSING							

SINAI COVENANT
Election: Israel as revelatory people of God (Ex. 6:7)
Revelation: Law reveals God's character

DAVIDIC COVENANT
Election: Davidic dynasty as sanctioned Kings
Revelation: Kingship reveals God's position

New covenant proclaimed

NEW COVENANT
Election: Believers in Christ as soteriological people of God
Revelation: Plan of salvation reveals God's provision

Christ: Fulfills covenant (combines aspects of revelation and salvation)

Son of God: God's Character
Messiah: God's King
Savior: God's Salvation

Note: for full discussion see John H. Walton, *Covenant: God's Purpose, God's Plan* (Grand Rapids: Zondervan, 1994)

IV.

Miscellaneous

Distances Between Old Testament Cities

	Ashkelon	Babylon	Beersheba	Bethel	Bethshean	Carchemish	Damascus	Dan	Haran	Hazor	Hebron	Jericho	Jerusalem	Joppa	Lachish	Mari	Megiddo	Memphis	Nineveh	Samaria	Shechem	Sidon	Susa	Thebes	Tyre	Ur
Ashkelon		900	36	48	87	454	178	139	519	117	36	57	44	32	21	653	80	269	726	60	63	155	1118	601	133	1070
Babylon	900		930	869	823	479	724	764	442	783	901	869	880	868	907	251	824	1172	264	845	847	779	218	1504	792	170
Beersheba	36	930		58	104	484	206	166	549	147	28	61	47	62	25	679	116	259	752	80	78	190	1148	591	176	1100
Bethel	48	869	58		47	423	145	105	488	86	31	12	11	32	40	618	50	303	691	26	22	129	1087	635	115	1039
Bethshean	87	823	104	47		377	92	59	442	40	78	45	57	59	86	572	21	349	645	27	26	82	1041	681	62	993
Carchemish	454	479	484	423	377		278	318	65	337	455	423	434	366	461	228	378	726	285	399	401	333	697	1058	346	649
Damascus	178	724	206	145	92	278		45	343	59	177	134	149	133	181	473	98	441	546	121	123	55	942	773	68	894
Dan	139	764	166	105	59	318	45		383	19	137	105	116	104	142	513	59	408	586	80	82	29	982	740	28	934
Haran	519	442	549	488	442	65	343	383		402	520	488	500	396	526	191	443	791	215	464	466	398	660	1123	411	612
Hazor	117	783	147	86	40	337	59	19	402		118	86	97	85	124	532	41	389	605	62	64	43	1001	721	29	953
Hebron	36	901	28	31	78	455	177	137	520	118		36	21	45	17	650	80	297	723	51	53	161	1119	629	147	1071
Jericho	57	869	61	12	45	423	134	105	488	86	36		15	43	44	618	54	307	691	32	26	129	1087	639	115	1039
Jerusalem	44	880	47	11	57	434	149	116	500	97	21	15		36	29	629	61	292	702	37	33	140	1098	624	126	1050
Joppa	32	868	62	32	59	366	133	104	396	85	45	43	36		37	372	53	301	548	31	36	112	1086	633	89	1038
Lachish	21	907	25	40	86	461	181	142	526	124	17	44	29	37		656	83	281	729	66	62	158	1125	613	136	1077
Mari	653	251	679	618	572	228	473	513	191	532	650	618	629	372	656		573	921	173	594	596	528	469	1253	541	421
Megiddo	80	824	116	50	21	378	98	59	443	41	80	54	61	53	83	573		348	646	25	29	75	1042	680	53	994
Memphis	269	1172	259	303	349	726	441	408	791	389	297	307	292	301	281	921	348		994	329	325	424	1390	332	402	1342
Nineveh	726	264	752	691	645	285	546	586	215	605	723	691	702	548	729	173	646	994		667	669	601	453	1326	614	434
Samaria	60	845	80	26	27	399	121	80	464	62	51	32	37	31	66	594	25	329	667		8	105	1063	661	77	1015
Shechem	63	847	78	22	26	401	123	82	466	64	53	26	33	36	62	596	29	325	669	8		107	1065	657	80	1017
Sidon	155	779	190	129	82	333	55	29	398	43	161	129	140	112	158	528	75	424	601	105	107		997	755	25	949
Susa	1118	218	1148	1087	1041	697	942	982	660	1001	1119	1087	1098	1086	1125	469	1042	1390	453	1063	1065	997		1722	1110	145
Thebes	601	1504	591	635	681	1058	773	740	1123	721	629	639	624	633	613	1253	680	332	1326	661	657	755	1722		733	1674
Tyre	133	792	176	115	62	346	68	28	411	29	147	115	126	89	136	541	53	402	614	77	80	25	1110	733		962
Ur	1070	170	1100	1039	993	649	894	934	612	953	1071	1039	1050	1038	1077	421	994	1342	434	1015	1017	949	145	1674	962	

Note: These distances are meant only to give rough estimates. They do not take terrain obstacles into account, though they do, for the most part, follow ancient routes (e.g., around the fertile crescent rather than across the desert).

Old Testament Weights and Measures

MEASURE	SYSTEM EQUIVALENT	METRIC	ENGLISH
Gerah	—	.6 g.	.022 oz.
Bekah	10 gerahs	6 g.	.22 oz.
Shekel	2 bekahs	11 g.	.4 oz.
Mina	50 shekels	500 g.	1.1 lb.
Talent	60 minas	30 kg.	66 lbs.
Royal shekel	—	13 g.	.5 oz.
Heavy talent	120 minas	60 kg.	135 lbs.

WEIGHTS

MEASURE	SYSTEM EQUIVALENT	METRIC	ENGLISH
Digit (width of finger)	—	19 mm.	3/4 in.
Handbreadth (width of hand at base)	4 digits	76 mm.	3 in.
Span (outstretched hand)	3 handbreadths	230 mm.	9 in.
Cubit (elbow to fingertip)	2 spans	445 mm.	17.5 in.
Long cubit	2 spans & 1 handbreadth	520 mm.	20.4 in.
Reed	6 cubits	2670 mm.	105 in.
Gomedh	2/3 cubit	300 mm.	12 in.

LENGTHS

MEASURE	SYSTEM EQUIVALENT	METRIC	ENGLISH
Log	—	.3 lit.	2/3 pts.
Kab	4 logs	1.2 lit.	2-2/3 pts.
Hin	3 kabs	3.6 lit.	1 gal.
Bath	6 hins	22 lit.	6 gals.
Homer	10 baths	220 lit.	60 gals.

LIQUID

MEASURE	SYSTEM EQUIVALENT	METRIC	ENGLISH
Log	—	.3 lit.	.32 qts.
Kab	4 logs	1.2 lit.	1.3 qts.
Omer	7 logs	2.2 lit.	2.3 qts.
Seah	6 kabs	7.3 lit.	1 pk.
Ephah	3 seahs	22 lit.	3/4 bu.
Lethech	5 ephahs	110 lit.	3 bu. & 3 pks.
Homer	2 lethechs	220 lit.	7-1/2 bu.

DRY

Rabbinic Writings
Torah–Written Law

WRITING	SECTIONS	DATES	CONTRIBUTORS	CONTENTS
MIDRASH	Halakah	100 B.C. to A.D. 300	Tannaim*	Legal sections commenting only on Torah
	Haggada			Narratives, homilies, and parables on whole Old Testament
BABYLONIAN TALMUD	Mishnah	A.D. 200	Tannaim	Digest of oral laws; interpretations of Torah by the Great Rabbis
	Gemara	A.D. 500	Amoraim	Commentary on the Mishnah by later Rabbis
PALESTINIAN TALMUD	Gemara	A.D. 200	Amoraim⁺	Commentary on the Mishnah
TOSEFTA		A.D. 100 to A.D. 300	Tannaim	Teachings omitted from Mishnah

*Tannaim: from Ezra, through Hillel, Akiba, and Meir, to Judah Hanasi
⁺Amoraim: The later Rabbinic scholars

Subject Index

Subject Index